Saint Francis & his Four Ladies

W · W · NORTON & COMPANY · INC · NEW YORK

BY THE SAME AUTHOR · The Universal Bead

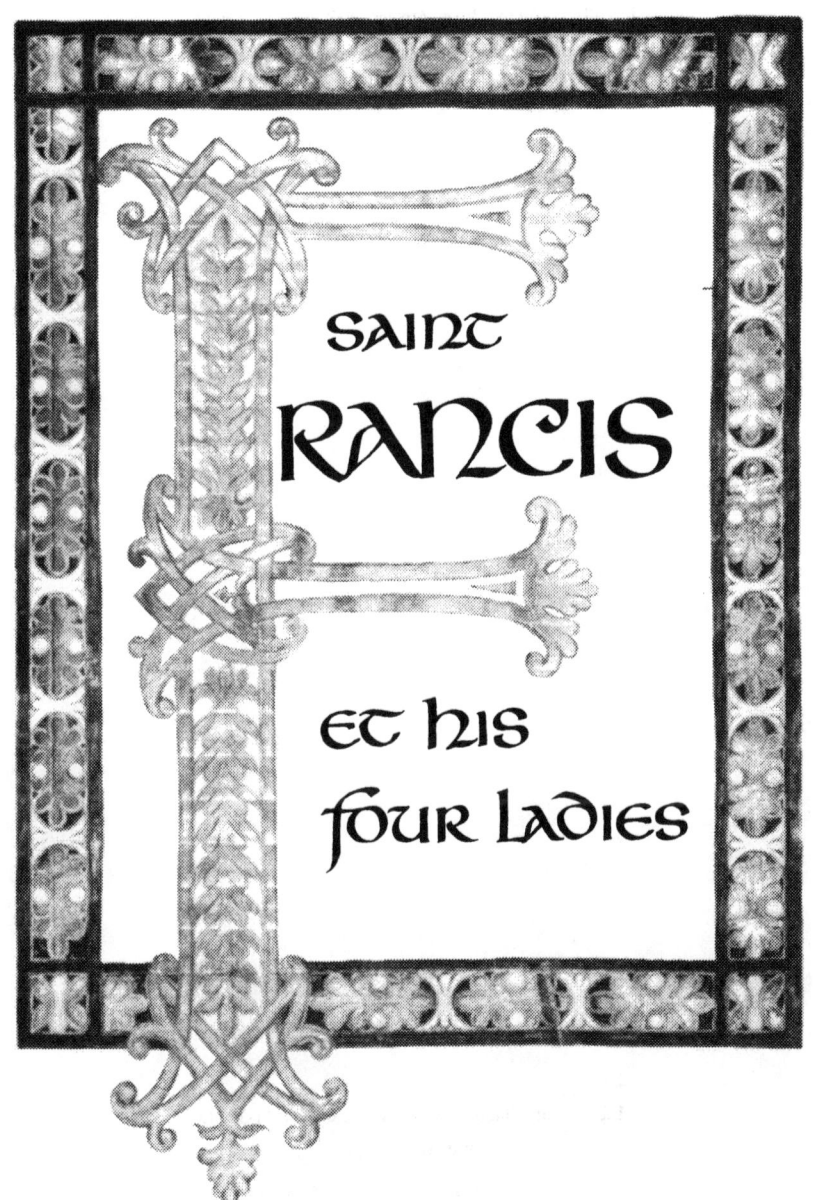

Saint Francis
et his four Ladies

Joan Mowat Erikson

FIRST EDITION

Copyright © 1970 by Joan Mowat Erikson. All rights reserved. Published simultaneously in Canada by George J. McLeod Limited, Toronto. Printed in the United States of America.

Library of Congress Catalog Card No. 71-127178

SBN 393 05427 6

1 2 3 4 5 6 7 8 9 0

OR Dorothy Day,
friend of poverty

CONTENTS

Preface	9
Saint Among Saints	17
Saint Francis of Assisi	39
The Lady Pica, his mother	53
The Lady Poverty, his wife	71
The Lady Clare, his daughter	83
Our Lady Queen of Heaven	101
Artist Saint	117
References	133
List of Illustrations	137

preface

THE traveler in southern Europe—Spain, France, Italy—will find himself quite frequently passing through small towns whose names are prefixed with "San" or "Santa," followed by the name of a saint. Inquiry will usually lead him to an old church which bears the name of this patron saint and around which the village perhaps originally clustered. With time, community life converges on newer centers, and daily business outgrows the old market place, changing town configurations and ongoing patterns of life. But one small town on a hillside in the middle of Italy stands apart because it seems to exist solely in honor of its greatest son, Saint Francis. The tremendous basilica, tiny isolated San Damiano, connected by crooked cobbled streets, tell one story only, and those who come to this shrine come for the most part only to hear it, to follow the well-known legend as made visual by the great murals within the basilica. When artists are of the stature of Giotto, Cimabue, and Martini, the legends are joined with the history of art.

The verified facts concerning the life of Saint Francis of Assisi, however, are few, and even the given dates are disputed.

PREFACE

Yet legend and his continuing presence have formed an impelling image which takes on greater stature as time goes on, as if in defiance of the lacking evidence.

What are our sources of information about Francesco Bernardone, born in Assisi in 1182? There are scant town records, a few verifiable dates concerning his dealings with the papal court, and the probable dates of some of the most important meetings of the chapter at the Porziuncula, the little chapel in the valley where the early Franciscans met. We have only few authenticated writings, since he dictated almost everything he wished to say to his followers, and much has not survived. Even the best known of his works, the prayer "Oh Lord, make me an instrument of Thy peace," so truly Franciscan in spirit, is only "attributable" to him. It was found in a Franciscan monastery in England.

After his death in 1226, one Thomas of Celano was commissioned by the Holy See to write his biography. Thomas was a Franciscan who had spent much of his life in Germany doing missionary work there. Some years later, after further materials had been gathered from those who had lived close to Saint Francis, Celano undertook to write a second version. However, in 1265, St. Bonaventura was instructed to write the definitive biography of Saint Francis, and shortly afterward an edict, demanding "all

PREFACE

other legends to be destroyed," was issued by the General Chapter in Paris. Only those writings survived this edict which had come into the hands of non-Franciscan monastic orders and had been given sanctuary by them.

Out of this residue of verified fact and beloved legend, the image of Saint Francis emerges.

The power of this figure is extraordinary. It has survived in our time obviously not because of a continuous body of literature, since much of the data cited became available to modern readers in translation only in the later half of the nineteenth century. The Franciscan order which he founded and the Poor Clares, who lived faithfully according to his precepts, have by their example undoubtedly kept the memory of his life fresh and vital for those who have come in contact with them. The literature itself, however, and even The Little Flowers of Saint Francis have not proven to be easily readable. Many translations are as awkward as the archaic forms of speech of the originals, and a certain "odor of sanctity" which pervades the record is too sweet for non-Catholic taste and perhaps for twentieth century Catholic taste as well, while the record of miracles is too pious for even those who are inclined to believe in the miraculous. But in spite of the cautious approach of much of the general public to this literature, the image

PREFACE

of the slight brown-clad saint tenaciously survives.

The town of Assisi itself has played an important role. Hundreds of thousands of travelers have come to visit the basilica, Santa Chiara, San Damiano, the ruined fortress on the hill, and the medieval gates; and some, no doubt, have become pilgrims, if ever so reluctantly, who carried away enduring ideas and unsettling values that colored and changed their lives.

The following reflections are the testament of such a traveler. Drawn back to Assisi many times, one becomes an amateur in the ancient sense of the word: a devotee of the Franciscan legend.

OF THE many people who were helpful in bringing about this book I would like first to express my indebtedness to Helen Post, who was my companion on my first visit to Assisi—long ago when the Via Francesca was still a dusty dirt road.

For the generous sharing of information and the loan of many books from her Franciscan library, I warmly thank Nesta de Robeck of Assisi. John R. H. Moorman, Bishop of Ripon and author of several books on Saint Francis, helped me to find material and I am grateful for his suggestions. Diane Lato made local inquiries about Umbrian saints possible by guiding me affectionately around a countryside she knows so well, and by acting as interpreter when my Italian failed me.

At Harvard, William Alfred provided me with a most detailed and helpful bibliography which led me to texts I would otherwise never have found. To Francis Smith I am indebted for encouragement and many enriching comments on the manuscript. Alice Wohl edited the manuscript with loving attention to detail, thus contributing immensely to its readability. Muffy Paradise contributed the hand lettered chapter titles and consulted with us on the layout. At the Pierpont Morgan Library Louise C.

PREFACE

Houllier was of great assistance in finding pre-Franciscan illustrative material which might visually evoke the spirit of the times. Finally, Ann Burt typed the manuscript with understanding and care. To all these friends I am most grateful. And one is always deeply appreciative of the support and applause of close relatives. My thanks to Kai and Erik.

I wrote this essay in San Fortunato de la Collina in a house which overlooks the Tiber valley and which on clear days offered us a distant view of Assisi. For this privilege I am grateful to Sally and Robert Fitzgerald.

Saint Francis & his Four Ladies

SAINT AMONG SAINTS

SLOWLY, and with some persistence, one can become acquainted with the better known of the saints, one by one, as they have been portrayed in paintings, stained-glass windows, and sculpture in chapels and churches. But this remains a somewhat haphazard procedure, for the stylistic clues which identify each figure are often obscure. Let us imagine a great fresco depicting the assembled haloed throng in Paradise—thousands of martyrs with their instruments of torture and death, groups of hermits heavily bearded and dressed in the skins of animals, long-robed monks and nuns in the varying habits of their orders, valiant knights and warriors, and numberless mystics, visionaries, and workers of miracles. We would perhaps readily recognize Saint Peter holding the great keys of the golden gate of heaven; Saint Sebastian, his naked body full of arrows; Saint Catherine with her wheel of torture; Saint Christopher bearing the Child on his shoulders; the evangelists carrying books. Only a student of symbols could hope to name more than a few of the individuals in the mighty gathering whom the Church has decreed to be among the elect. Yet one slight figure in this great host will undoubtedly stand out clearly for many onlookers, be they Catholic, Protestant, or otherwise persuaded or nonpersuaded, as though they had already met him somewhere: and this is the small brown-clad Saint Francis. He will be as in Cimabue's painting, standing a little apart looking somewhat detached, with perhaps a few wild flowers in his hand or a small bird perched on his shoulder.

This, then is the Saint Francis that the nineteenth century rediscovered, whom it enshrined in gardens and found convincing and appealing. We may well ask why of all the throng of saints this unspectacular man should have remained so memorable, for many of the things that he did others also accomplished even more sensationally, and he died early—of weariness and illness, to be sure, but not a martyr's violent death. He founded a great order of monks and nuns which grew phenomenally in his own short lifetime and which remains established throughout the world today; but so also did Saint Benedict, Saint Bernard, and others, both before and after his lifetime. They are all there in our fresco—somewhere. If we can recognize them, we may well view them with respect and awe, for their lives were great in dedication, in knowledge, or in leadership. The slight, haloed figure of Saint Francis, however, is not as awe-inspiring as it is moving. He is highlighted only by his utmost simplicity, by a totally convincing humility.

This feeling only increases with knowledge about his life and with each vignette in the Little Flowers which his followers gathered to remember him by and to pass on to us. What he did and what he was seemed to them so miraculous, both in his lifetime and in retrospect, that the little collection is colored with a pervasive sense of the supernatural. Yet Francis himself comes through as so literally down to earth, so sure in his sense of purpose, and yet so

SAINT AMONG SAINTS

courteous and humble, that the world has been won by his person rather than by either the miraculous acts attributed to him or by the proofs of sanctity recounted by his brothers.

How then was it possible for Saint Francis to become officially sanctified and yet to remain unique? Were there models for him to measure himself by—or to disengage himself from? Were small boys in the twelfth century surrounded by images and legends of saintly characters which might serve as models of perfection? And, above all, if Francis were to become so unforgettable, with what strengths, what gifts was he especially endowed?

In order even to consider possible answers to these queries, let us imagine our fresco before he took his place in it, and then look at it once more with the eyes of the little boy Francesco Bernardone, and focus our attention on those saints whose legends he might have heard.

Aside from those on whom the Church was founded (Saint Mary, Saint Joseph, Saint Elizabeth, Saint John the Baptist, the Apostles, and Saint Paul), the first officially recognized saints were the early martyrs who died for refusing to worship Roman gods and emperors. And they were truly an amazing phenomenon, these converts to a faith in a crucified God who inspired one another to face lions in the arena and various other grim deaths and who by their astonishing example of courage increased their own ranks day by day. Their persecutors, if we are to judge by the legends, bent every effort to devise new and sadistic forms of torture and death in order to subdue the spirit that united them. It was all recorded gruesomely and graphically for the faithful in the early churches—Saint Pantaleon with a lion, Saint Vitus in a cauldron, Saint Margaret with a dragon, Saint Erasmus being disemboweled by means of a windlass, and so on. Even as today we peruse the tabloids for minutest details of dreadful accidents and brutal murders, in the

Stoning of Stephen

SAINT AMONG SAINTS

Middle Ages young and old were aroused and impressed by the gory particulars of martyrdom. The paintings and descriptions, we must assume, were intended to induce self-searching as to one's faith and courage and to inspire the cultivation of these virtues. But though we may be offended aesthetically by the artistic efforts to depict the suffering of these saints, we must acknowledge that by these portrayals alone we have come to know about them, and we cannot well deny this overwhelming evidence of hope and fortitude.

That a great demand for saints existed in the early days of the Church is easy to understand. During long years of persecution the heroism of the martyrs gave their fellow Christians the courage and strength to persevere. We are told that

> Canonization in the age of the martyrs was a spontaneous act of the local community. There was no occasion for any kind of judicial investigation. The members of the local churches were well known to one another and when one of their number was put to death by the Roman authorities the circumstances were sufficiently plain to require no investigation. A martyrdom was a great occasion in the life of the community. When a Christian was put in prison or taken before the magistrate his conduct, his fortitude, and his punishment were matters of vital interest to all his fellows.[1]

This sanctification by public acclaim resulted initially in the inclusion of the name in a list or "catalogue" of saints; shrines and churches were built in their honor, and legends commemorating their deeds were amassed and preserved by word of mouth. That great reverence was felt for the remains of the martyrs is recorded in this tribute by his friends to Saint Polycarp, who was burned to death in A.D. 156.

> We afterwards took up his bones which are more valuable than precious stones and finer than refined gold,

and laid them in a suitable place; where the Lord will permit us to gather ourselves together, as we are able, in gladness and joy, and to celebrate the birthday of his martyrdom for the commemoration of those that have already fought in the contest, and for the training and preparation of those that shall do so hereafter.[2]

As the demand for such valuable relics increased, the methods used to acquire and to clean, dry, and distribute the bones became, to our present-day sensibilities, both unsavory and horrifying.

Even when the Church was finally established and martyrdom remained only as the final lot of missionaries, the number of saints accorded veneration by the populace continued to increase apace. Why were they so eagerly acclaimed? The relics which had miraculous properties were, of course, a partial reason for the demand, but undoubtedly martyrdom as such offered an awesome ideal, an aspiration to spiritual and physical heroism, which was too high for ordinary men. Most Christians, confronted with an all-but-impossible ideal, experienced the world as a miserably evil place. And since the devil, replete with horns, cloven hooves, and a tail, was as real and as constantly in wait to snatch souls as God was to redeem them, human beings desperately needed the special intercession of more familiar and less formidable saints.

And so the catalogue increased until thousands of names were recorded among the elect. By 993, the length of the list began to concern the Vatican, and access to this record was regulated by stricter procedures. By the twelfth century, sainthood was bestowed only by canonization, a word derived from the insertion of the name of the new saint into the Canon of the Mass. Thus, according to Bellarmine, canonization became "the public testimony of the Church concerning real sanctity of some deceased persons."

For young Francis, growing up in Assisi around the year 1200, there were in addition some local saints of Umbria who were household words. For example, San Feliciano, the first bishop of the city, was said to have set up a cross on a hillside where the faithful could "pray and praise Him in the morning, in the noon day, in the evening," and who died on his way to martyrdom in Rome. Then there was San Savino who, at his trial in the forum in Assisi, coolly smashed an image of Jupiter made of coral and gold. For this his hands were cut off, but he finally converted the Prefect himself, who was later beheaded, while San Savino was scourged to death in Spoleto.

The Cathedral in Assisi is named after San Rufino, who became bishop there. He also was arraigned in the forum for refusing to burn incense to the Roman gods and was thrown into a fiery furnace. From this he emerged unscathed, but although tortured further, he remained true to his faith and was then finally tied to a block of stone and drowned in the river.

These stories, here briefly outlined, were recorded in minutest detail. In each case the questions and answers in the procedures are given with the full Italian flare for drama. Take, for example, the trial of Savino by Venustiano Augustale.

V.A. Who are you?
S. Savino, a bishop and a sinner.
V.A. Are you slave or free?
S. A slave of Christ, free from the devil.
V.A. By what authority do you secretly preach to the people to the end that they abandon their gods and follow a dead man?
S. So you think our Savior Jesus Christ is dead?
V.A. Yes, he was killed and buried.
S. Don't you know that on the third day he arose?[3]

And so the brave scene develops through the breaking of the image, the conversion, and the final martyrdom of both leading

Adoration of the Lamb by the multitudes

characters. Perhaps the event was re-enacted in the city piazza near the fountain or in front of the handsome façade of the cathedral for the edification of the twelfth century Assisans. If so, little Francis was surely there to watch.

Each of the hilltop towns that dot the Umbrian countryside claims local martyred saints after whom the old churches are named. The legends have grown dim, many too dim for retelling, but who would erase the portraits and the names of the elect in the edifices that testify to the sanctity of their lives and their heroic deaths? Moreover, local saints are cherished communal property who are naturally expected to take immediate and personal interest in their own towns and who are on intimate terms with their erstwhile neighbors. For saints, having been human, may more surely be counted on to sympathize with the ever-present human problems, griefs, and burdens and will lend an ear and speed the humble prayer to the throne of Grace.

Not all of these thousands of listed saints are accredited martyrs and certainly not all credible saints. But even though they became an embarrassment to the Church, so that finally the lengthy lists were pruned and the way to official sainthood was made narrower and harder, the rules proved to be easier to change than the people; and the saints have remained more real to simple souls than has the Trinity, as any visit to a village church can verify.

There are saints on our great fresco who do not bear any resemblance to townspeople. They are the long-haired, bearded men, half-draped in ragged cloth or the skins of animals. These are the hermits and the desert fathers who withdrew from the world to live a life of isolation and contemplation. There were hermits in the caves of the mountainsides of Umbria, and later in his life Francis came to envy them their retreat from the world, their immersion in prayer and praise.

SAINT AMONG SAINTS

One story Saint Francis must have heard repeatedly as a child, for it seems to find echoes in his later life, is the story of Saint Fiorenzo, the hermit. This lonely saint found his life of austerity and isolation too hard and prayed for a companion to join him. One day a bear appeared at his door and

> bowed its head to the ground and showing no sign of ferocious intent gave him to understand that it had come to pay homage to the servant of God.[4]

The saint called his new friend "Brother Bear," and they lived out their lives in warm companionship.

He may also have heard of the desert hermit, an old man, who was found to be weathering the cold desert nights by sheltering a lion in his cave with whom he slept in gratefully shared warmth. Saint Francis may have followed a traditional image when, in his inclusively generous manner, he later dubbed *all* animals "brother" and thus, as the legends tell, won their simple trust.

As this group of hermit saints is presented in our fresco, we

are strongly reminded of the description in the Bible of Saint John the Baptist, who

> wore a garment of camel's hair, and a leather girdle about his loins and locusts and wild honey were his food.[5]

Like the lion's friend, these are men of the desert, not hermits of Umbria, and they are as gaunt as the diet just described would suggest. Something of their history has been recorded by one Rufinus of Aquileia, and their wise, salty, and eminently practical sayings were eventually collected in a lengthy Latin folio. It is, of course, not possible to state explicitly that young Francis knew this literature; but since there are a number of pre-thirteenth century frescos and paintings depicting such hermits in the area of Assisi, it is reasonable to assume that he had heard about them. They were, in any case, the spiritual forerunners of his order—in a very real sense his desert fathers. This is, in brief, their story. In the fourth century as the Roman Empire crumbled, a large group of men began to occupy the desert areas of Egypt, Palestine, Arabia, and Persia. They lived in cell-like huts, earned a meager livelihood by weaving baskets, and although isolated from one another, met regularly for worship. In the silence of the desert these Christian hermits lived an austere life of contemplation. We would call them ascetics, but in so doing, we should remember that this word is derived from *ascesis* and referred to the training of the athlete and that therefore these men aspired to becoming *athletae Dei*, "athletes of God." With them asceticism was not reckoned a virtue in itself but as a discipline undertaken in order to develop strength and renunciation, gentleness and humility. They were criticized for their solitariness, these self-exiled men, and for ignoring "the giant agony of the world." But their sayings suggest that they were well aware of the dangers inherent in their chosen isolation.

SAINT AMONG SAINTS

> Unless thou first amend thy life going to and fro amongst men thou shall not avail to amend it dwelling alone,[6]

says Abbot Lucius, and the Abbess Matrona adds:

> It is better to have many about thee, and to live the solitary life in thy will than to be alone and the desire of thy mind be with the crowd.[7]

But at the same time they believed firmly in the training of facing oneself alone. "Go, sit in thy cell, and thy cell shall teach thee all things," Abbot Moses of Scete says, and "all things" included charity as evinced in solicitous hospitality and complete generosity.

> A brother came to a certain solitary: and when he was going away from him, he said, "Forgive me Father for I have made thee break thy rule." He made answer and said, "My rule is to receive thee with hospitality and send thee away in peace." [8]

To find in these desert isolates such gentleness and courtesy and above all such humility and tender concern for one another marked them as saintly for the witnesses who described their way of living. But years of such living could result in a very real unworldliness as shown by one recorded remark: "Tell me, I pray thee," says an aged father to a visitor from distant parts, "how fares the human race; if new roofs be risen in ancient cities: whose empire it is that now sways the world?"

Since, however, they aspired above all things to learn humility and since they are revered as having achieved great excellence in this virtue, let me quote some of the recorded "Sayings" which illustrate their manner of teaching. The first is attributed to Abbot Pastor:

> A brother said: "I have heard tales of a certain brother that do not edify me." The old man heard him and looked upon the ground and picked up a little straw and

> said to him, "What is this?" He answered, "A straw." And again the old man gazed at the roof of the cell and said, "What is this?" "It is the beam that holds up the roof." "Take it to thy heart that thy sins are as this beam: the sins of that brother of whom thou dost speak are as this poor straw." [9]

And as one would expect, delusional temptations also lurked in such loneliness as testified to by the experience of a man who even remains humbly anonymous.

> The devil appeared to a certain brother, transformed into an angel of light, and said to him, "I am the angel Gabriel, and I am sent unto thee." But he said, "Look to it that thou wast not sent to some other, for I am not worthy that an angel should be sent to me." And the devil was no more seen. [10]

But perhaps most impressive in their earnestness and simplicity were the parablelike actions of the great black figure, the wise and gentle Abbot Moses.

> A Brother in Scete happened to commit a fault, and the elders assembled and sent for Abbot Moses to join them. He, however, did not want to come. The priest sent him a message, saying: "Come, the community of the brethren is waiting for you." So he arose and started off. And taking with him a very old basket full of holes, he filled it with sand, and carried it behind him. The elders came out to meet him and said: "What is this, Father?" The elder replied: "My sins are running out behind me, and I do not see them, and today I come to judge the sins of another!" They, hearing this, said nothing to the brother, but pardoned him. [11]

These stories are offered here at some length because they illustrate the method of teaching by parable that Saint Francis later perfected. They have the same simple dramatic appeal that his actions had for his superiors as well as for his brothers and his audience. Such acted parables remain in the memory when oratory and discourse fade and blur. For who can ever forget the Abbot Moses and his basket full of holes, dragging his way to a hearing called in order to condemn a brother? And how can one account for the present-day devotion to Saint Francis which is expressed in the presence of his figure in gardens and bird sanctuaries, unless the account of his dramatic ability to make his "sisters the birds" listen to his preaching were still moving and meaningful after more than seven hundred years? Less well known, but perhaps even more truly in the spirit of these hermit forefathers, is Saint Francis' humbled acknowledgment of failure when he, too brashly, undertook to repeat this previous success.

> Brother Masseo has said that he was present with the Blessed Francis when he preached to the birds. Rapt in devotion, Francis once found by the roadside a large flock of birds, to whom he turned aside to preach, as he had done before to another lot. But when the birds saw him approaching they all flew away at the very sight of him. Then he came back and began to accuse himself most bitterly, saying, "What effrontery you have, you impudent son of Peter Bernardone"—and this because he had expected irrational creatures to obey him as if he, and not God, were their creator.[12]

Although Francis was drawn to the solitary life and later retreated often to hermitages for rest and renewal from his demanding duties, he also inherited the legacy of the saintly monks and nuns who preceded him. They appear in our fresco like trees in a forest so uniformly clothed that we have difficulty identifying the individuals. There are, however, great ones among them—the founders of orders which were important in their time of origin and are still flourishing today. These gowned men and women are rather monochromatically clothed in garments appropriate to the

SAINT FRANCIS AND HIS FOUR LADIES

Tomb slab of monk

simple people of the period when their orders were founded and when, for poverty's sake, one comprehensively covering garment had to suffice. In this great monastic group we can perhaps isolate Saint Benedict. He is dressed in black, and we may remember the importance first of his efforts to preserve in his monastery early documents that might otherwise never have survived the Dark Ages, and second of his emphasis on the virtue of physical labor. In this he stands with the great Augustine; both their orders were founded on the precept that men, especially men of God, should band together to live a *vita mixta* of action and contemplation "wherein the love of truth doth ask a holy quiet, and the necessity of love doth accept a righteous busyness"—a precept the later Franciscans wholly endorsed.

Bernard the Cistercian and his saintly brothers are there in white, as well as Domenic, the friend of Francis, and many, many more. There were, of course, thousands of monks living in monastic groups as early as the third and fourth centuries with centers in Egypt, Arabia, and Palestine. These differed from the desert fathers in that their lives were far from solitary; they lived, in fact, rigidly disciplined lives under firm hierarchical direction. For centuries monastic life was the road to both sanctity and religious respectability,

SAINT AMONG SAINTS

since its recognizable habit and its rigorous conventions gave meaning to self-chosen poverty and a life of piety when the average citizen was sometimes at a loss to draw the fine line between saints and madmen.

And, indeed, how could one tell the difference between religious obsession and pious devotion? For there was surely often a very blurry distinction not only for the citizens but also for the ecclesiastical authorities who had to make the final judgment. The Church was glad to canonize men who actively revived and assiduously supported the Church, but in all ages the people's imagination has been aroused to enthusiasm by excesses of asceticism, extravagant humility, and of course, the miraculous.

In Saint Francis' time there certainly was, then, an image in people's minds as to the visible attributes of saintliness and some of the more humbly honest of the saintly aspirants admit to having actually courted public acclaim. The Blessed Angela of Foligna writes:

> During my whole life I have studied how that I might obtain the fame of sanctity. I diligently made an outward show of being poor, but caused many sheets and coverings to be put down where I slept and taken up in the morning so that none might see them.[13]

And Jacopone da Todi, a poet of Saint Francis' era, who fought a valiant fight but did not quite make the fresco, writes:

> *Very far my feet have strayed*
> *From the road the saints have made!*
> *Yes! far enough away, and yet I wind*
> *A coiled hypocrisy about my mind*
> *And strive to show myself to all mankind*
> *With shining sanctity illuminate.*[14]

And indeed in his conspicuous sanctity he carried poverty and humility to the excessive length of going about filthy, as did, of course, many others, which naturally resulted in their being "rejected of men"—even at some distance.

Even though the color of the garments of the monastic saints in our fresco varies somewhat, their relationship is visibly affirmed by their robes. They stand together, an order of men and women who support one another in a style of life. In contrast to this are those saints, vaguely described as mystics, who are difficult to recognize either by clothing or by symbol. There is good reason for this, for their whole effort in life was directed to becoming as inconspicuous as possible—"make yourself small, very small" was one of their guiding precepts. In fact, even small is too big. The great mystics have diligently sought to attain a "noughting" of the soul, a complete immersion in the will of God and in His love which would be higher and somehow beyond the active life of virtue. To this end poverty and asceticism, detachment and charity were essential elements in their lives, and to these more or less visible attributes must be added great tenacity of purpose and of courage.

Summed up, much of all saintliness somehow sounds like a stark negation of the world and of life. True saints have spoken of "denying the world, the flesh, and the devil" and have used the phrase "leaving the world" when entering a dedicated order. This is probably why they are sometimes thought of as dull and drab and as emanating an unattractive air of sanctity. But saintliness is, of course, impossible to describe or define. Since it is of necessity a process of becoming and of being in a constant state of transcendence, there are few aspects of saintliness one can capture in words—or symbols or colors. Therefore, who can know in whom among this throng in our fresco such mystic life was centered? Perhaps some of the courageous martyrs were also advanced in the ways of mysticism. Nor does anyone have any idea how many of these wise and humble men of the desert achieved that "selfnoughting" to which they aspired. Any number of those, in turn, who sought the seclusion of the cloister may have quietly found peace of soul unacclaimed and have become very small indeed.

No doubt young Francis Bernardone venerated his saints, even as he revered his heroic knights of chivalric legends. And, indeed, in contrast to the somberly clothed monastics stand the warrior saints arrayed in shining armor. Saint Michael dominated this group as well he might, since he is the winged, sword-bearing archangel of judgment and also the revered patron saint and ideal of crusaders and medieval knights. Saint George is of his company with dragon underfoot; as is Constantine, holding high the cross, and Wenceslaus, the warrior king, who is better known to us as the good king who "looked out on the feast of Stephen" and with his page cared for a poor man bringing him "flesh and wine and pine logs." What little boy's eyes would not be drawn to the splendid trappings and the stance of courageous resolve, for figures who have fought the good fight for the enduring glories have always been necessary to young dreams. Righteous wrath does have its appropriate place in human affairs, and every Faith has had need of valiant defenders against evil in the form of the infidel or of mythical beasts.

Such ideal heroes command victorious battlefields, honors, and titles. The mystics, on the other hand, by active, self-chosen renunciation, heroically deny the material values of the world. Giving up perishable wealth, they choose to own everything by being attached to nothing—rather than wielding temporary power, they elect to bend with humility. It has been—it still is—an ironically unassailable position.

Now let us approach the small brown figure as portrayed by Cimabue, asking ourselves what the singular strengths and gifts of this "instrument of Thy peace" may have been. There is a stur-

SAINT AMONG SAINTS

diness in this face but also a great sensitivity. The eyes are active and searching and yet express an inwardness, an air of introspection. One is aware of firmness and yet of a pervading humility. Perhaps it is the firmness that leads one to believe that his stamina and energy were derived from his consistent "willing of one thing" —an inspired persistence.

We must, however, gain an idea of the pattern of his life and of the historical and social matrix in which he grew up, in order later to select certain items for detailed inquiry in our search for a measure of his stature. The following chapter, then, will present a brief account of his life.

SAINT FRANCIS OF ASSISI

THE composite which has become known as Saint Francis' story—a series of dramatic happenings held together by the image of a unique personality—has been told and retold in greatest detail by many competent writers, and there are volumes upon volumes of comment and controversy pertaining to Franciscan dates and details. The sketch offered here provides only a bare outline—a time chart and map to orient us as to sequence and place.

Francesco Bernardone was born in 1182 in the hill town of Assisi in Umbria. Umbria lies in the center of Italy, encircled by mountainous areas and watered by the Tiber. The wide fertile valley itself is edged with hills, each topped by the towers of a walled medieval town. From Assisi it is possible to look across fields and trees to Perugia, the dominant city of Umbria. Between these towns there was constant strife in medieval times, each commune being fiercely independent.

Pietro Bernardone, Francis' father, was a well-to-do cloth merchant, at a period in Italian history when the merchant class was beginning to exert influence and a new degree of power. His mother, Pica, was from Provence.

SAINT FRANCIS AND HIS FOUR LADIES

Few facts are recorded concerning Francis' early youth, but the legends claim that he was a high-spirited, generous lad who liked to dress well and lead the revels in Assisi. We do know that in 1202, when he was twenty years old, he fought against the Perugians in the battle at Ponte San Giovanni, a crossing of the

Tiber. He was taken prisoner and held in Perugia for one year. On his return to Assisi Francis remained for some time ill with a fever.

In 1205, he decided to join a band of young Assisans who were being recruited to fight under Walter of Brienne and the Papal forces against the Empire. But at Spoleto, not many miles from his home, he had a dream in which a voice demanded, "Francis, whom is it better to serve, the Lord or the servant?" Understanding that this question meant that he was about to enter the service of the wrong rule, he then returned to Assisi, leaving his knightly trappings and his horse behind him.

SAINT FRANCIS OF ASSISI

He next undertook a pilgrimage to Rome to visit the tombs of the Apostles. There, outside Saint Peter's, he exchanged clothes with a beggar and for the first time experienced the lot of the really poor. Upon his return home he became aware of the beggars of Assisi and of the plight of the most deprived and despised among them, the lepers. Overcoming his repugnance for the sufferers from this horrifying disease, he befriended them and made them his special care.

San Damiano is a small chapel on the outskirts of Assisi. In Francis' day it had fallen into disrepair, but he used to wander off there to pray. There he heard the figure of the crucifix say to him, "Francis, go and repair my house, which as you see is wholly a ruin." He immediately went home and then taking with him some valuable cloth, set off for the market in nearby Folignia. There he sold his goods and came back to San Damiano, offering the money to the caretaking priest for the repair of the church.

His father, Pietro, on hearing of this transaction, came to find

him and ordered the return of the money. Francis refused to obey and was then called before the Bishop of Assisi, who commanded him to obey his father. He complied by doing so but also stripped off all his clothing, saying that these garments also belonged to Pietro Bernardone, whom he would no longer regard as father.

He then undertook to rebuild San Damiano and two other chapels by hand, begging in Assisi for his bread and for the stones with which to build. At this time too, in spite of the jeers of the townspeople, he began to preach, and soon he was joined by a small group of followers.

When the brothers had become twelve in number, they decided to go to Rome in order to get the approval of the Pope. They received a verbal confirmation of their order from Innocent III and called themselves Friars Minor. Their rule was the literal word of the Bible, "Take no thought for tomorrow," "Take nothing with you," "Tell the good news of the kingdom," "Care for the sick, the poor, the distressed." The group wandered and preached, centering their lives initially at Rivo Torto and then later at the Porziuncula, one of the small chapels in the Tiber valley that Francis had repaired.

In 1212, when Francis was about thirty years old, he was approached by Clare Faverone, who had heard his preaching and wished to dedicate her life to his rule. She was then about eighteen years old, the beautiful daughter of a prominent nobleman. He established his second order under her direction and installed these nuns in San Damiano.

The years 1212 to 1215 were taken up with teaching and traveling through Italy. His fame had grown to such a degree that he was being hailed as a saint by the populace, and the number of his followers increased astonishingly. In this time two missionary journeys were undertaken, one to Syria, which failed because of storms at sea, and one to Spain, from which he had to turn back because of illness.

In 1215, he attended the General Council in Rome convoked by Innocent III for reform in the Church and for the Crusade. It is at this period in his life that he probably wrote his "Letter to All Christians," a letter reaching out to men everywhere and urging a new realization of Christ's message. Also at this time the "order of Penance" or the Third Order was organized to include all those who wished to observe his rule but were tied to home and family.

The Porziuncula indulgence was granted to Francis in 1216 by Honorius III in Perugia. Those who entered the Porziuncula were to be "freed from all guilt and penalty both in heaven and on earth from the day of baptism till the hour of their entering into this church." This indulgence met with such disfavor from the papal court, since it was felt that it would serve to decrease the value of the important and sought after Crusade indulgence, that Honorius limited it finally to one day a year, the day of the consecration of the chapel.

By 1217, the fraternity had spread so extensively over Italy and other countries that the General Chapter at the Porziuncula undertook to appoint Provincial Ministers. At this time, too, it was decided to establish provinces in France, Spain, Portugal, Germany, and Hungary, and probably in Syria. Francis elected to go to France, since he spoke the language of that country; but he only got as far as Florence, where Cardinal Ugolino detained him, having a premonition that the order would not hold together without its leader.

The Chapter of Mats (so called because of the wattle huts in which the brothers were lodged) was held in 1219, attended by five thousand friars. At this meeting the dissension in the fraternity began to be truly outspoken. The bone of contention was the rule of poverty, which Francis and his close following maintained must remain absolute; whereas, a large group of brothers was in favor of the relative poverty of other orders, which sanctioned communal property, books, and learning and the safeguards and privileges accorded to traveling monks. The chapter disbanded without conclusively resolving these issues, but nevertheless, with unified plans for further missions. Francis himself took charge of the mission to the Mohammedans in Egypt.

This mission Francis actually carried out, proceeding to Damietta, where the Christian army was encamped, and finally successfully crossing the lines to talk to the Sultan Malak-el-Kamel. Although he did not convert this sultan, he was courteously treated and returned safely to the Christian camp. He left the Christian army after the fall and sack of Damietta, which disgusted him, and he spent some time wandering through the Holy Land. Returning to Acre, he heard that the dissension in the order had increased, and he hurried back to Italy.

There he found confusion and disunity, and it soon became apparent that the rule must be revised. A way of life that was possible for a small group of mendicant friars was proving inappropriate for an order with thousands of members.

The chapters (meetings) held in the following year (1222–23) were again absorbed by the problem of rule revision. Francis repeatedly tried to reword the original form without forfeiting its pristine simplicity. The revised rules pleased no one, and dissension grew. Francis then withdrew to the Rieto hermitage, and a final form was drawn up and approved by Honorius III.

Francis had been ill since his return from Syria, suffering from an infection of his eyes which worsened and was most painful. He

undertook, nevertheless, to spend six weeks in retreat at the mountain hermitage of La Verna, accompanied by several brothers. Here he received the five wounds of the stigmata on his hands, feet, and at his side. Following his return in slow stages to the Porziuncula from La Verna, Francis became increasingly ill and almost blind. A hut was built for him in the garden at San Damiano, and for some time the sisters cared for him there. During this stay he dictated the "Canticle to Brother Sun."

Hearing of the condition of his eyes, Cardinal Ugolino sent for Francis to come to Rieto to seek medical help. There the cauterization of his upper cheek and ears was undertaken to relieve him of pain. This, however, failed, and he grew increasingly weak. He was then taken to Siena for further help and finally brought back to Assisi. He died at the Porziuncula in 1226 at the age of forty-four.

At the time of his death he was revered as a saint not only in Umbria but wherever the Franciscans had traveled on their far-flung missionary journeys. Within two years after his triumphal funeral, he was canonized by Pope Gregory IX who, as "Cardinal Ugolino," had been his staunch friend for many years.

That the populace should have acclaimed him as a saint is not surprising. There was obviously a charismatic quality to his presence which endeared him to all, and the integrity and consistent focus of his work won respect. But his position in relationship to the Holy See had often been so marginal that his unqualified acceptance by that body must remain, indeed, astonishing.

His actions were in many ways provocative enough, and his friars on their missionary journeys were often accused of heresy. In outward appearance and in their way of life, they were fellow travelers of other, heretical reformers of their time.

The twelfth and thirteenth centuries were dominated by a calling for a return to the simplicity of the early Church. This new energy produced a large group of religious reformers whose aim was to break away from the established order which represented pomp, wealth, and authority but also, to an extreme degree, corruption and degradation in its priesthood. Like Arnold of Brescia, Saint Francis was in protest against the luxury and political power of the Church. Like Peter of Bruys and the Apostolics, he longed to re-establish the original purity of worship and denounced earthly possessions, and he was in general accord with the way of life of the Humiliati and the Waldensians.

The Church has, on the whole, been tolerant of much extravagance in pious behavior, of fast-induced hallucinations, even of sensuous descriptions of divine love, doubtless unwilling to condemn in an area where certainty is so difficult. But she has of necessity been less tolerant when any novel pious activity seemed to be leading toward rebellion in her ranks, a lapse in morality, or a challenge of doctrine. She has thus undoubtedly been misled into destroying on occasion some of the world's most saintly people and honoring others for reasons of polity.

Saint Francis neither openly criticized the established order of the Church for its pomp and vainglory nor for the prevalent depravity of the clergy. By consistently maintaining standards of simplicity and devotion in his own life, he highlighted these deficiencies and silently focused attention on them. It was characteristic of him that he avoided challenging the authority of the Church and demanded of his brothers that all priests be treated with deep respect. He also invariably turned to the highest authority available for guidance and sanction. He early sought out the Bishop of Assisi, then Pope Innocent III, and finally Cardinal Ugolino. In personal confrontation he won the trust and respect of these high dignitaries and then serenely proceeded on his own idiosyncratic way.

Independence, however hazardous, is necessary to allow the

time and leeway for spontaneous improvisation—than which there is no higher form of art—and in this Saint Francis was a skilled and disciplined artist. His spirit demanded much freedom of action which made him unwilling to anchor himself or his brothers in permanent dwellings. His great strength lay in unfailingly using his energies and talents for reconciliation—and he had enormous energy and a rare combination of special talents. A dedicated son of the Church he was, but no outside authority could mold that combination for the purposes of ecclesiastic power.

THIS, then, is the general background of life data which is necessary for the more specific concerns of this study.

In spite of the reticence of his biographers, one finds oneself aware of St. Francis' deeply courteous relationships during his lifetime with several feminine figures. Four of these ladies will be introduced in the chapters which follow. But there is another perhaps related side to this saint which has for some people blurred his image. I mean a rather mysterious feminine quality which in the eyes of many has characterized him as a mild and passive figure. And yet was this very femininity not one of the sources of his peculiar strength?

If we speak of Saint Francis as an artist, and unquestionably his dramatic and poetic abilities were outstanding, we must ask how these gifts were nourished in his youth and later manifested in his maturity. For to bring talent to creative fruition requires a merging, a consolidation of the inherent polarities within the artist and every man—the masculine and feminine elements of his nature. From the balancing of these elements, accompanied by the preservation into adulthood of the glowing curiosity and creativity of childhood, comes the sure wholeness of the uniquely great.

Is it possible to trace the feminine elements in this man's na-

SAINT FRANCIS OF ASSISI

Saint Francis of Assisi

ture and some of the qualities of the creativity which emerged?

Saint Francis, it is true, was always surrounded by men. His youth is described as gay and gregarious in the company of the young blades of the city. No one will suppose that the "revels" alluded to in the story of his life were exclusively masculine affairs, but by and large much of his time was probably spent with young men and in his father's place of business. His father, we may gather, was a strong man, generous, but willful and ambitious for his oldest son. To defy him took manly courage, such courage as Francis had exhibited in armed combat.

Since he founded an order of men and lived with them in close association, he was seldom alone after the first years following his conversion. The small group of early followers increased steadily, even alarmingly, until thousands of brothers convened for the biennial chapter meetings at the Porziuncula.

The vow of chastity made it prudent to avoid all contacts with women, and Saint Francis explicitly forbade his brothers to talk with women and recommended that when an exchange of words was necessary, they should keep their eyes on the ground. To maintain chastity of action and thought was apparently a constant battle, and that very real character, the devil, seemed ever ready with lewd temptations.

But we must assume that living in a celibate group surely makes a certain polarizing of the masculine and feminine components of "human nature" necessary. Within a large group of men there will be those who become administrators and intellectual leaders and those who have a greater capacity for empathy and tenderness and who develop the ability to take more care.

Men who are dedicated to obedience—obedience to their superiors as well as obedience to the inner voice—must also be able, we are told, to wait and listen, to be open and receptive to directive and admonition. The humility necessary for such response and the capacity for "waiting on God" (*en hypomene*) have been for centuries considered unmasculine, if not outright feminine virtues, perhaps because they are those feminine attributes most foreign to men of action—to men's men.

Since Francis was so specially beloved by his brothers for his "miraculous" ability to "read their minds" and since they record so many examples of his tender care for their welfare, we should examine what we know of his childhood for possible models of such maternal behavior. And in spite of the careful editing imposed on his biographers, who no doubt felt obliged dutifully to "keep their eyes on the ground" both when talking to and about women, we may find clues in the record suggesting the identities of the real and the symbolic feminine figures who first sustained and later played their supporting roles in his greatest dramatic creation—his own life.

the Lady Pica his mother

EVEN great men have mothers and yet how often do we read in biographies, "little is known of his mother," as though she had served only to produce and nurture the physical existence of the man as an infant. And yet her role is intimately involved in her son's most impressionable and formative years. Saint Francis is no exception to this rule. About his mother almost nothing is recorded. We are told only, and here all accounts agree, that the Lady Pica probably came from Provence.

More is known about his father, Pietro Bernardone, the prosperous cloth merchant. Since his business entailed extensive travel, it is credible that he should have had contacts in southern France and that he might have brought his wife from there to Assisi. That there were well-established trade lines to France is attested to by the fact that before the birth of Francis there was already a Via Francesca in Assisi, skirting the city and connecting the main approach with the little chapel of San Damiano, which was to become so important in the life of Saint Francis and Saint Clare, and then proceeding to the nearby market town of Folignia.

SAINT FRANCIS AND HIS FOUR LADIES

The son that was born to the Lady Pica in 1182 was first named Giovanni Bernardone and was christened in the Duomo of San Rufino, the patron saint of Assisi. Perhaps his father was away at the time of his birth because the story is told that he later renamed his son Francesco, and by this nickname he was known to his family and friends and became known to the world. And so a gay nickname, "little Frenchman," was destined to become one of the most revered names in Christendom.

Lacking evidence, then, we can only conjecture in an effort to reconstruct a possible image of Pica Bernardone. And this we do in the hope that future historians may begin to provide us with some information concerning the first important feminine influence in a man's life.

The mother of Francis had grown up in the south of France sometime during the latter half of the twelfth century and had come to Assisi with her dowry of Provençal riches. Was she a merchant's daughter whom Pietro Bernardone had met on his travels? Did she know by experience anything of courtly life? Not even the legends give us a clue to her background, but we do know that in a foreign land she taught her small son her tongue and the songs of her country. Francis' brothers were to record more than once, as if it were a matter of very special interest, that he spoke and sang in the French language.

But we are justified in assuming that the cultural dowry which the young French wife shared with her son was far richer than this, for Provence was flowering with an new freedom of spirit which found expression in all the arts but especially in music and literature. Perhaps the inspiration for this spiritual upsurge had come from the Near East and Spain by way of the Crusades, but it had undoubtedly been nurtured by the great queens of France who dominated court life during this period. Under their

auos que no no sabetz. Tan
len ter sauenon ensems. Lo
senz el prez e labeutatz. Eiz
ftancx cors canc bona fos
natz.

E sim fueill eu tener clam. So
uassals de los bons seingn
ors. E nomen soi del tor Lais
satz. Quel nesig cors ab que
batrill. Fris con tra leis eras
mi quetz. Ve dis que lam
son uele remis. De mans
en con briers eu passatz. En
quem fora desesperatz.

C ero de cabrol ode dam. Si
pretz entendes uel a mors.
Cui era soi ado mesfaitz. mas
uos ma dompna non assaill.

L ans numerces
car non uetez. Los mals qui
en trac nuls planetz nul gems.
Que fas la nueg em soi col
gatz. Qieu non puesc estar
en patz.

S i per dieu en sots estam. No
us platz quem traspas La do
lors. Que m austra sinon

pensatz. E reu merses o zgoill
nous tfail. Epassatim si no
sentez. Con es lois fredutz
esems. Can de seruizi non
uengutz. Sellm que ney mor
trebaillatz.

E sim tenez prez e iitam. Eno
ual forsa niualors. Nom ual
es humilitatz. Si sa pos
eshen. Vostres mang estim
destrignetz. Qui mays me
uolgra ser tezems de mas
mutz ode reuelatz. Quen
tal trebailla foi titutz.

P er uos dompna quem de
strignetz. E uer ben en esse
tegems. De mas mutz ode
reuelatz. Anz auissi foi uiste
zlatz. Dompna merey car
pen satz. Com eu non foy ros
tempos forsatz.

G iraut de burnel.
S il cors nom lus tan oreg.
E mal son grit non la fra
ing. Enun chan taret soul.
Romez uis quem safring
na. Si non es for satz. En un

SAINT FRANCIS AND HIS FOUR LADIES

influence the idea of "courtesy" was introduced into the relationship between men and women, and we shall call Francis' mother the "Lady Pica," for it was in Provence that the very idea of the "lady" was born. This title claims our attention because it incorporated an idea of great importance to Saint Francis and one that colored all his relationships with women.

It was not necessary to be a lady of the court to take part in this new wave of literature and music. Certainly the Lady Pica must have been familiar with the music and poetry of church liturgy, for the Crusades brought a great resurgence of religious feeling and expression. This was evidenced by the building of churches, attendance at services, and the many great processions and pilgrimages. Pilgrimages, which were enormously well attended, were popular as an appropriate outlet for religious zeal and provided at the same time stimulating social events, an opportunity to travel, to meet all sorts and conditions of people, and to talk, to recite verse, and to sing. The focus of entertainment was the "jongleur" or "troubadour" who was "at home in every abbey, castle or cottage, as well as at every shrine." The early troubadours composed as well as sang their songs, and their repertoires included a tremendous mass of poetry known as the *Chansons de Geste,* which extolled the heroic exploits of knights. They sang about historical deeds and recounted the rhymed stories of great heroes, the most celebrated being the *Chanson de Roland,* that warrior's song of courage, loyalty, and valor. "Chanted by every minstrel—known by heart, from beginning to end, by every man and woman and child, lay or clerical," this is the song of the twelfth century. This is a story of action, a story of men involved in battle with a common enemy. Their bond is an idealized loyalty, their saintly hero the invincible Saint Michael.

That Francis knew and loved the romances of chivalry and

Knights in Battle

that his imagination was fired by them, we know both by his early deeds and by the words which he later used in reprimanding a young novice. It is recorded that he appealed to the examples of "Charles the Emperor, Roland and Oliver, and all the paladins and strong men"—an extraordinarily unmonkish admonition.

But there are no women in these tales of valor. It was the troubadours of the twelfth century with their songs of courtly love who first extolled chivalrous conduct as an ideal relationship between men and women. The *chanson d'amour* followed a set pattern. The lover, separated from his lady by barriers of all kinds, expresses his desire, grief, resignation, and constancy in lengthy variation. The troubadours and young nobles composed and sang these songs, which were then spread by the jongleur and all who cared to sing. There were perhaps a hundred or so such troubadours known by name in the latter half of the twelfth century. This was vernacular poetry of a high order of both emotion and intellect.

The courtly epic or romance also became popular at this time, and the master of this literature, Christian of Troyes, evoked for

THE LADY PICA

his era the legendary world of King Arthur and his Knights of the Round Table. These stories of Lancelot, Perceval, Gawain set up standards of chivalrous behavior which were intended to be relevant for all human relationships, friend, foe, or lady, and extolled a striving for greater perfection in and a higher ideal of daily conduct. In these romances women play an important role, always "on hand to transform and ennoble man," who strays into "immature battles and passions." Through his relationship with the woman the man "gains access to his own soul, to the deeper layers of his 'heart,' his sorrowing quest for his 'queen' makes him wiser, more sensitive, more scrupulous as a person." Christian of Troyes was writing for the ladies of the court and their knights. The real lot of women in the twelfth century, of course, in no way generally reflects these sentiments. But it was a phenomenon of the literary history of the century that the romances and the songs spread throughout Europe with amazing rapidity and were translated into many languages.

These stories, verses, and songs of the Knights of the Round Table were the vehicles by which the ladies of the courts in the cities and in the provinces instructed society in courteous love. If the earlier songs had extolled prowess and loyalty among men, the later songs took up the praise of exploits of greater refinement and restraint and a more feminine delicacy. Courteous love was, to be sure, a form of ceremonial performance, but like all ritualized behavior of the elites of any period, it was also a tremendous social force.

In order to gain some idea of the sense for Francis of courtly love, of the courtesy which he extended to all creatures and all things, it is essential to try to understand what was meant in the medieval world by the word *love*. Interestingly enough, defining the meaning of this much-abused word was a preoccupation of medieval writers, and both poets and theologians devoted their attention to this theme.

It is important, to begin with, to realize that romantic love between the sexes as we understand it had no place in early feudal society. Feudalism was based on cohesive bonds between vassal and lord, underling and master, bonds of fidelity and humility joined with those of fidelity and responsibility. Intense and warm relationships could and indeed did flourish as well as sharp hatreds when a vassal turned traitor. Strong feelings, vows, and the kiss of peace, rather than written contracts, sealed relationships. The fidelity of the vassal extended quite naturally to the ladies of the lord's household.

Marriage was a legal social contract between families and an ecclesiastical sanction to propagate offspring, and any nonsense as to personal preferences was not considered.

Amor (love) had two aspects, *cupiditas* and *caritas*. Cupiditas defined a relationship based on the use or misuse of another person for the indulgence of one's passions. Such abuse could conceivably be part of any relationship. Carnal love was simply lust and remained a sin even between man and lawfully wedded wife.

Courtly love, then, and the adulation of a woman as "a lady," which found its form in ceremonial behavior both in daily life and in literature, was an innovation midway between carnal (cupiditas) and spiritual (caritas) love. It found its highest expression in the veneration of the Holy Virgin—even as it could also serve as a cover for simple adultery.

Caritas, on the other hand, was the "bond of all order, the trace of the Holy Spirit in the universe" (Saint Aelred). Sublimated love and formalized aggression were the mainsprings, the cohesive elements in the social order. But the deepest emotion expressed in early medieval writings is that of the love of man for man.

Of caritas Saint Anselm of Canterbury says that it must be taught to man by man so that it may be purified, grow, and consolidate, and this lesson can best be learned from a friend (*amicus*). Friendship became identified with an exalted relationship and could be described in terms of ecstasy "with God as the goal" and as a "foretaste of heaven." "He who abides in friendship [says Aelred] abides in God."

Small wonder that life "in the world" seemed to the thoughtful and concerned a hopeless struggle against pervading sin. One should emphasize "thoughtful and concerned," because the Church inclined toward leniency in matters of carnal sin for the many and even supported pre-Lenten carnivals and Gaudete in Advent. Within the patterns of the feudal system, one could nourish the bonds of fidelity which flowered into courtesy, but passion was out of bounds for all who dared hope for heaven. What a release, then, for the human spirit the drama of courtly love provided as acted out by the nobility for the participation of all in fantasy and dream. The ritualization of sublimated passion in a great outburst of song and pageantry, in mock court ceremony and verse gave rein to aestheticism and sensualism in a life style which elevated both women and men.

In the monasteries to which young men flocked looking for a haven from this world's besetting sin, William of Saint Thiery describes the "heavenly paradise of monastic friendship." And Aelred, too, refers to his cloister in terms of a paradise. Walking through it, he sees that; "the brethren sitting there are a sweet and loving crown of flowers. He marvels at the leaves, flowers, and fruit of each tree; in all that multitude there is not one whom he

SAINT FRANCIS AND HIS FOUR LADIES

does not love and by whom he does not trust that he is loved. He is filled with joy that surpasses all delight which this world can give." [1]

The monasteries, orderly and hierarchical, the members, bound by vows of poverty, chastity, and obedience, these we understand were nevertheless a safe and clostered place within which love (caritas) could be nurtured and sustained. A loving community life marked the early years of the Franciscan order—and the search for such relatedness in communities of a manageable size has continued to spark the founding of Utopias ever since. Saint Francis, however, transcended the formalism of his time by combining caritas and courtesy in a manner both personal and universal.

When we bear in mind his Provençal heritage, the stories of Francis' early life take on a greater richness of meaning. For it is said that he won friends with his gaiety and song and that—perhaps in imitation of the court life he had heard about—he liked to dress in rich clothes, to eat and drink with other young men, and to join them in fighting his city's battles, even though such battles sometimes ended in defeat like the engagement against neighboring Perugia in which it is recorded that he was captured and imprisoned. From the illness which followed this episode, Francis may have learned how devastating affliction and weakness of the body can be for the spirit of a man. He later came to call his own body "Brother Ass," which combines a kind of courtesy with humor, for he demanded untiring service of it.

But he was solicitous and gentle with his brothers, and one is tempted to suppose that for this intuitive understanding of how to care for people, there was a model in his childhood and in his home. Somewhere he learned the art of tenderness. And where else

Blanche of Castile, Saint Louis,
author and scribe

would he have encountered and learned his extraordinary style of solicitude and courtesy? Two legends illustrate this empathetic caring for others. Out of love of ascetism and an excess of piety, some of the friars at times used to fast even beyond the standard imposed on them by necessity. Francis never approved of this. Once, we are told, while they were still at Rivo Torto

> it fell on a night, all the friars being at rest, about the middle of the night, one of them called out saying, "I am dying! I am dying!" Whereon all the friars woke up amazed and affrighted. And the holy father rising said, "Rise brothers, and kindle the light!" And when it was lit, he said: "Who is he that said 'I am dying'?" The brother answered: "It is I." And he said to him, "What is the matter, brother? How dost thou die?" And he said, "I am dying of hunger." Then the blessed father caused the table to be laid straightway, and like a man full of charity and discretion, ate with him lest he should be put to shame by eating alone; and, by his will, all the friars ate likewise. For that brother, and for all the other friars who had newly turned to the Lord, used to afflict their bodies even beyond measure. And after the meal the holy father said to the other friars: "Dearest, I bid you, each one, consider his nature, because though one of you may be able to sustain himself on less food, yet I will that another who requires more food shall not be bound to imitate the first in this thing, but shall, considering his own nature, give his body what it requires, so that it may be able to serve the spirit. For we are bound to beware of superfluity of eating, which harms body and soul, so also must we beware of too great abstinence, nay, even more since the Lord will have mercy and not sacrifice. . . . Therefore I will and command you that each of our brethren, according to our poverty, satisfy his body as it shall be necessary for him.[2]

THE LADY PICA

On another occasion this tender consideration was shown when Francis realized that one of the older brothers was afflicting himself more than was good for him.

> ... and he said within himself, "if that brother would eat some ripe grapes early in the morning I believe it would do him good." And as he thought, so he did. For he rose on a certain day, very early, and called to him, that friar privately, and led him into a certain vineyard which was near the dwelling. And he chose a vine whereon the grapes were good to eat, and sitting near the vine with that friar, began to eat of the grapes lest the brother himself should be ashamed to eat alone. And while they were eating the friar was cured, and together they praised the Lord.[3]

Courtesy remained his lifelong code in his relationship with all men and women. "Know, beloved friar," he says,

> that courtesy is one of the attributes of God, who giveth His sun and His rain to the just and to the unjust, through courtesy; and Courtesy is own sister to Charity, the which extinguishes hate and keepeth love alive.[4]

It is evident in all his almsgivings, for such giving was never regarded merely as an occasion for doing good. Always included was attention, a meeting of the eye, compassion, and an embrace. In fact, with Francis no one was *merely* a man, nothing was *merely* a thing, nothing was even *merely* ordinary.

No example of his touching courtesy is more moving than his words to Brother Fire, when in the last year of his life the medical men in Rioto decided that cauterization was necessary to improve his infected eyes and relieve his pain. Weak as he was at the time, as the irons were being brought to a glow over the fire, he said, "O Brother Fire, whose beauty exceeds that of every creature created by the Most High, resplendent for our use, be piteous to me in this hour; deal gently with me for the love I have always had for you in the Lord. Grant that He may temper the heat so that I may be able to bear it."

Perhaps something of this quality of courtesy can illumine for us the stories of his relationship to animals which were remembered and recorded because they speak of a very special kind of grace. He preaches to the birds, "My sisters . . . be ye ever mindful to give praise to God"—and he reforms the wild wolf of Gubbio, "Come hither brother wolf," which the wolf does obediently.

And there are the wild doves which he tamed, a deer that he met and talked with in the woods, a nightingale whom he joined in the praise of God. And then, memorable because it conveys something of Saint Francis' simplicity and humility, as well as the astonishing power attributed to him—the story of the "ungovernable ass."

THE LADY PICA

Brother Tebaldo once told us something that he himself had seen. When Saint Francis was preaching one day to the people of Trevi, a noisy and ungovernable ass went careening about the square, frightening the people out of their wits. And when it became clear that no one could catch it or restrain it, Saint Francis said to it: "Brother Ass, please be quiet and allow me to preach to the people." When the donkey heard this it immediately bowed its head, and to everyone's astonishment, stood perfectly quiet. And the Blessed Francis, fearing that the people might take too much notice of this astonishing miracle, began saying funny things to make them laugh.[5]

If we see as a possible source of Saint Francis' style of caring both a maternal model and the experience of having been treated courteously as a child, we may in the same way see in the quality and form of his preaching a reflection of a childhood model, namely, the *Jongleur de Dieu*. None of his sermons survive, and this is not because his followers were negligent about recording their content. Rather it was that his extraordinary presentation seemed to envelop the words. One writer notes rather plaintively,

> Whereas I can remember every word of the sermons of others, the words uttered by holy Francis alone escape me. If I commit any of them to memory they do not seem to me the same that fell from his lips before.[6]

His biographer does tell us, however, that "His words were kindly but fiery and penetrating; his voice was powerful, sweet toned, clear, and sonorous," and he made "ardent gestures and movements." On one occasion when preaching before the Pope and the Cardinals, he became so carried away by his enthusiasm that he began to dance. But there was no laughter, for his preaching conveyed the devotion and conviction of the life of the man, as well as the truth of his words. The highest dignitaries were, in fact, moved to tears.

SAINT FRANCIS AND HIS FOUR LADIES

There was actually much singing and playing of instruments, on lute and pipes and the vieille, in those days in Umbria, and popular songs and melodies also served as dance tunes. Confraternities of singers, singing guilds, met in the evenings in the piazzas of the Italian towns and sometimes marched in procession singing hymns of penitence or adoration—the early Lauda in the vernacular. These were songs about the life of Christ and the saints set to easy melodies. As a matter of fact, in the type of melody and rhythm there was often little to differentiate secular from religious music. Francis encouraged such minstrelsy, which played an important role in the earliest versifying in the language of the people. And he eventually did much more than this, for his own writings are the first great poems in the Italian language.

And Francis sang with his "sweet-toned and sonorous voice." If he learned the songs of the troubadours at home, which is probable since he sang "in the French language," he did not hear them only there, for the songs of these minstrels were widely sung in Italy. But we may well asume that, having heard the original songs from his mother's lips, he sang them with a special, nostalgic knowledge.

> Then he would sing, so full was his soul of melody. He would begin softly, then the song would become louder and French words would pour from his lips as though he were rendering into words other sounds which his ears heard.[7]

Saint Francis sang all his life. On his death bed, no longer able to see the stars and the flowers, he still sang and asked his sorrowing brothers to sing to him. It was pointed out to him that this was unseemly because "the men of this city think thee a saint," and they asked one another, "How is it he thus openly rejoices, he who

THE LADY PICA

is about to die and should be thinking of his death?" But Francis was above playing roles of any kind:

> Leave me, brother, to rejoice in the Lord and in His praises and in my infirmities, for by the grace of the Holy Spirit working in me, I am so united and wedded to my Lord that by His mercy I can well be merry in the Most High.[8]

If we assume that Francis' devotion to chivalry and courtesy and his love of song can be traced to his mother Pica, we may also surmise that his father personified, or at any rate encouraged, all the manly virtues. This we can deduce from his final quarrel with his son. Pietro Bernardone had apparently been proud of his gay, fun-loving son of the early days and had not begrudged him whatever was needed to support him and his friends in their feasting and fun. But he was violently upset by this same son when he began to disassociate himself from his young friends and seek the companionship of beggars. At one point during the rather long, drawn out quarrel between Francis and his father over the stolen cloth, we are told that while he was away from Assisi, he had his son locked up in his house in order to keep him under control. And here the Lady Pica again enters the story briefly, allegedly to release him, "for she deeply sympathized with her son's aspirations."

One could wish to know much more about the relationship of the young wife from Provence with her first-born son. That she taught him the "French speech" might indicate a nostalgia for the sound of home, and it may be that it gave her solace in the small and isolated Italian city of Assisi to share the songs and legends of her homeland with him. But if there is to the image of every mother not only a unique aspect grounded in her culture and personality, there is always also a superpersonal image of motherhood which is related to the religious concepts of the time. And we may well remember the role which at that very time in history, France, the country of his mother's birth, played in the unprecedented cultivation of reverence for the Madonna. From this dowry of literature, music, and faith, her son perhaps received more than she knew, and one is inclined to trace in Saint Francis' courteous relationships with the other ladies who were part of his life, and indeed his courtesy to all men and to all things, a warm reverence for the Lady from Provence—his mother.

the Lady poverty his wife

HIGH in the ceiling of the lower basilica of Saint Francis at Assisi and not too easily visible is a remarkable fresco depicting a ceremony attended by an audience of overawed angels. It is Christ Himself who gives in marriage to a young monk what is probably the least bridelike figure in the history of art. The young monk is Saint Francis and his bride, the Lady Poverty. They stand on a rock, and he seems to be placing a ring on her finger, while the figure of Christ appears behind and between them with his eyes on Francis.

The most arresting figure is that of Lady Poverty herself—gaunt, pale, clothed in rags, yet imaginatively suggesting a disguised enchantress. A mass of thorns is placed at her feet, and two small street urchins are taunting her—one about to throw a stone, the other menacing with a stick. But behind her, silhouetting her hexagonal halo, is a flowering bush of roses. The Ladies Chastity and Obedience are in attendance, and the central group is surrounded by angels and a few other figures whose identity is perhaps know only to the artist to whom this work is ascribed—the incomparable Giotto.

SAINT FRANCIS AND HIS FOUR LADIES

Now the vow of chastity, obedience, and poverty was in no way original with Francis. It had been the vow of monks and nuns for centuries, but there was something about Francis' concept of poverty which was indeed new and which shook the foundations of monastic life. With his characteristic, impetuous literalness, he meant by poverty owning nothing—except one ragged garment to cover nakedness, and that only for the sake of decency and perhaps survival. His understanding of the word poverty precluded security of life in a sturdy building shared with others and the additional assurance of daily food, be it ever so simple. Life for his friars was to be lived from moment to moment in complete trust, giving "no thought to the morrow"—just as it was described in the Gospel. Like Francis' other ideas, this extreme concept was disconcerting to the society in which he moved and on which he and his brothers were dependent for day-to-day sustenance. But Francis' whole life was a dramatic questioning of existing values, a highlighting of hypocrisy: arresting, disrupting, embarrassing. It was, however, impossible to ignore him—and once he had gained attention, he moved rich and poor alike to tears and sometimes to song.

Why did Francis curse money so violently, call it dung, and treat it as such? Nothing aroused his anger more than the suggestion that a friar had touched a coin. We know that his home had been an affluent one, his father being a successful merchant. The legends suggest that he knew and took part in this business of his father's and that he was free in spending the profits. In this he was apparently encouraged. Money as such had gained a new status in the twelfth century, and bartering even in Umbria was no longer the chief method of trade. Goods, being perishable and space-taking, cannot be preserved for long, but money can be hoarded and loaned—a new and dangerous temptation which the

Marriage of Saint Francis
and Lady Poverty

SAINT FRANCIS AND HIS FOUR LADIES

Church, though it frowned on usury, was unable to curb. The growth of the cities gave impetus to this new economic system, greed was prevalent, almost symptomatic; and as trade grew, the disparity also grew between the enormously wealthy and the poor.

But Francis was no student of economics, and one may be reasonably sure that these signs of his times influenced him only insofar as inequalities became more flagrant. It is much more in tune with his nature to suppose that as his need grew to be more inclusive in his relationships with his fellow men, he recognized possessions and money as symbols of a most formidable barrier. Poverty, deformity, illness, and in his day particularly, leprosy, which combined all three, were the afflictions which made brotherhood among men impossible. Not until he had grappled with this problem of affliction and overcome his sensitive revulsion from dirt and disease could he be free and universally related. In the testament which he wrote shortly before his death, he says,

> The Lord gave to me, Brother Francis, thus to begin to do penance. For when I was in sin it seemed very bitter to me to see lepers, and the Lord Himself led me among them, and I showed mercy to them. And when I left them what had seemed to me nauseous was changed into sweetness of body and soul.[1]

The legend is, as always, more dramatic. As he rode home to Assisi one day, he met a leper on the road. Reacting with his customary revulsion, he prepared to throw the beggar a coin. Then overwhelmed with compassion and shamed by the condescending gesture, he jumped from his horse, courteously handed the man the money, and embraced him.

Having experienced this "sweetness of body and soul," he began to make this essence part of a more lasting good. Breaking barriers by means of renouncing wealth suggests a mere negation

THE LADY POVERTY

which was foreign to his nature. Francis' strength lay in staunch affirmation. So, troubadour that he was, he created a noble lady to whom he could swear allegiance. This lady, feared and despised by all, he would make his wife and serve with courage and fidelity —the Lady Poverty.

All the imagery of chivalry and courtly love was then evoked to give this allegorical lady reality for Francis and his friars. No service was too servile to perform at her injunction; indeed, service to her was an honored privilege. Did not the great ladies presiding over tournaments throw to their knights their scarves and the sleeves of their fine garments to wear in jousting? So with an equal loyalty would the friars wear ragged, patched habits in their knightly enterprises for Lady Poverty's sake. Was she homeless and a beggar? So would they be in order to be worthy of her company. By their very squalor, then, they were knighted and in her presence ennobled. The *Sacrum Commercium*, written in 1227, the year of Francis' death, vividly dramatizes this picture. The author is unknown, but the tone is authentically that of the early Franciscans.

> How the Blessed Francis made Diligent Search for the Lady Poverty
>
> Wherefore the Blessed Francis, as a True Follower and Disciple of the Savior, gave himself up from the beginning of his Conversion with all his Heart, with all his Strength, and with all his Mind, to seek and to find, to have and to hold the Lady Poverty, dreading no Adversity, fearing no Evil, sparing no labour, shunning no suffering of the body so only that he might come unto her to whom the Lord had given the Keys of the Kingdom of Heaven. Like an eager explorer he began to go about the highways and byways of the City, diligently seeking her whom his Soul did love. He asked of those who stood

> about. He questioned those who met him, saying: Saw ye her whom my Soul loveth? But his speech was dark to them as an alien tongue, and, not understanding him, they answered: We know not what thou sayest: speak to us in our own tongue, and we will answer thee. For there was not at that time any word or sign in the languages by which the Children of Adam could discourse together of Poverty. They hated her then as they hate her now, nor could they speak with patience to one who sought her.

So Francis approaches the Great and Wise who answer him curtly

> What is this new doctrine which thou bringest to our ears? Let this Poverty be on you and yours. And Francis replies, "Blessed art Thou, O lord God, who has hid these things from the Wise and Prudent and revealed them unto Babes."

Francis then finds two old men in a field and inquires in the language of courtly love:

> Tell me, I beseech you, where the Lady Poverty dwells, where she feeds her flock, where she takes her rest at noon, for I languish for love of her.

They answer that she "has passed this way often"—and he must ascend the great high mountain where she dwells. But he must put off "Garments of Pleasure and lay aside every weight and the sin which besets thee" because only "free from trammels" can he attain the great height.

He and his companions hasten to the mountain where they "behold my Lady Poverty on the topmost pinnacle." They climb valiantly to the top where she receives them kindly.

> So from the Throne of her Neediness, the Lady Poverty presented them with Blessings of Sweetness. "Can it be that you seek me who am poor and needy, tossed by the tempest, and bereft of all consolation?

THE LADY POVERTY

Francis begs the Lady Poverty to remain with them forever:

> "Thou art Queen of the Virtues—the Faithful Companion of Christ in earthly life" and you are praised by Him, "Blessed are the Poor in Spirit, for theirs is the kingdom of heaven." To these words my Lady Poverty, with joyful heart and cheerful mien and most sweet Voice, made answer . . . "your words are dearer to me than Gold and Precious Stones and sweeter far than Honey and the Honeycomb."

Then Lady Poverty tells them her story:

> I am not new [*non sum rudis*—"raw or new"]. In Paradise I was in Man, and of his Essence when he was naked. I was joyful exceeding, entertaining him at all times, for possessing nothing he belonged wholly to God.

When, however, Adam, aware of his nakedness, made himself an apron of leaves of the fig tree, this was a sin against Lady Poverty, for he was then stripped of the robe of Innocence; and when he then proceeded to make garments of the skins of animals, "death had come into the world." Then the Lady Poverty became a Wanderer Upon Earth until the coming of Christ, who exalted her and whose constant companion she became. The Apostles undertook her protection, but following them came times of trouble, war, envy, and struggle for the acquisition of wealth.

The Lady Poverty then praises Francis and his brothers: "You seem to have abandoned Everything and to have freed yourselves from all Burdens." They beg her to come with them, to which she agrees.

On arrival at their chosen place of rest for the night, a play full of irony is enacted, wherein she asks to be shown the oratory, cloister, chapter house, refectory, kitchen, dormitory, and stables —the whole inventory of monastic installations. They have nothing to show her—"We are weary—let us first eat." She requests water and cloth to wash her hands. They produce a broken earthenware vessel for water and offer the use of the habit of one the brothers on which to wipe her hands. Their food is three or four crusts of barley bread served on the grass and a basin of cold water in which to dip the dry crusts. She asks for a knife to cut the bread, "which verily is hard and dry," but they can only suggest that she use her teeth. Finally they show her their cloister—the summit of a bare hill below which stretches the wide world. All of this brings great joy to the Lady Poverty, who has tested them and found them constant and blesses them and begs them to persevere in their loyalty.

Francis, however, was not satisfied by a definition of poverty which focused solely on the lack of this world's goods, nor would he tolerate morbid self-pity among the brothers. He knew well that a display of conspicuous destitution could signify pride of piety just as surely as ostentatious display, a pride of possession. Poverty should be only the outward and dramatic expression of true humility—the heartfelt lowliness of the "poor in spirit." One had to be married to Poverty in the world of things and in that of ideas. Through obedience one must learn to surrender personal preferences, intellectual conceptions, and the proud separate sense of selfhood and ownership—the love especially of reputation. Sensing this danger in his order with the precision of a surgeon, he put his finger on what he felt to be the greatest source of a new ungodly pride in monastic life, namely, learning; and he focused his censure on books. Those who were ordained could have breviaries, and they should read to and teach their brothers; but the unlearned should say their prayers and do their work, preaching the simple precepts of the gospel—repentance, love, and praise. This was more important than learning, and books were indeed often mere possessions.

THE LADY POVERTY

In time—in Francis' own lifetime—a rift in the brotherhood developed over this injunction. There were learned men among his followers, and the times were rife with curiosity and desire for knowledge. Other orders gloried in their learning; the brothers became restless and jealous. The rule of complete poverty also became a problem as the order grew. Too many monks were begging, this preferred fare became scarce, and complaints increased about the improvidence of these wandering friars.

In his consternation over these stresses and outright quarrels, he once cried out, "Who are they who snatch my Order and my brethren out of my hands? If I come to the General Chapter I'll show them what they will get." [2] And we can be grateful that these hot, unsaintly words slipped by the censoring recorders, for though Francis never acted on this impulse, it shows us a very real person torn by anger. Francis Bernardone was not a man humbly born nor one who had acquired a sense of personal inferiority. He was born privileged and talented, and humility was not a cradle gift but a hard-won virtue. He knew the taste of power, for his charismatic leadership attracted crowds of followers. He once admitted, "There is no prelate in the whole world who is so much feared as the Lord would make me to be feared, if I so wished it, by my brethren." He knew, indeed, his power. "But," he continued, "the Lord has granted me this grace that I wish to be content with all, as he that is least in the Order." [3]

And so he transferred the power to others and sat at their feet during the stormy chapter meetings (tugging like a child at their robes if he wanted to interject a word into the discussion), in this way eloquently demonstrating his purpose and his will.

To the so-called Spirituals who persisted in his lifetime and afterwards in following Saint Francis' rule literally, the devotion to the Lady Poverty was the outward, visible sign of spiritual life, a "sacrament of liberation." The great Franciscan poet, Jacopone da Todi, gives expression to their positive sense of this Lady and the freedom they inherited through her:

> *The earth and all the plants that grow,*
> *The trees, and all the fruits they show,*
> *The very beasts, my yoke that know—*
> *All in my homestead I unite.*
>
> *The running waters, lake and sea,*
> *And all the fishes swimming free,*
> *The birds in windy air that be,*
> *These are the stuff of my delight.*
>
> *Since to God's will my being clings,*
> *I am the possessor of all things:*
> *So many feathers have my wings,*
> *To heaven it is an easy flight.*

Not only did Francis struggle to keep his Lady Poverty from being betrayed by those of her knights who could not resist the lure of the riches of learning, he valiantly opposed the construction of edifices to house them and fine chapels and churches in which to worship.

He had formed a mendicant order, and so he wished it to remain. He laid down this rule for them that if some benefactor gave them land on which to build a shelter—which he permitted since Umbrian winters are frigid—they were first to obtain permission from their bishop and his blessing:

> Let them go and make a great trench in the circuit of the land which they have received for building the dwelling and let them set there a good hedge as their wall, as a sign of holy poverty and humility. Afterwards let them make poor little houses of wattle and daub, and some little cells in which from time to time the friars may pray and work, for greater seemliness and to avoid sloth. Let them also build small churches, for they ought not to make great churches, neither to preach to the peo-

ple nor for any other reason, since their humility is greater and their example better when they go to other churches to preach. And if at any time prelates and clergy, regular or secular, come to their dwelling, the poor little houses, the little cells, and the tiny churches will preach to them, and they will be more edified by them, than by many words.[4]

Small wonder then that, when on his return from the Holy Land he found that the order in Bologna had built a large chapter house, he was deeply angry. Impetuously he rushed to the building, climbed upon the roof, and began throwing down the roof tiles. Only a message from the Bishop, telling him to stop, that this was property of the Holy See, made him desist—but he would never enter the place. In their blundering way those who loved him continued after his death to build monuments to his memory which negate all he taught. And so we see the great basilica, an imperial mausoleum, constructed shortly after his death as an appropriate burying place for the Poverello, and the tremendous building that now completely encloses his little, poor Porziuncula.

What irony! No doubt the Lady Poverty grieves on her mountaintop—although some of her knights continued to enter at least into verbal combat for her—as did Brother Giles.

> When Brother Giles once came to Assisi, the friars took him round their new home, showing him the splendid buildings which they had put up, and apparently taking great pride in them. But when Brother Giles had carefully looked at them all, he said to the brethren: "You know, brethren, there's only one thing you're short of now, and that's wives!" The brothers were deeply shocked at this; so Brother Giles said to them: "My brothers, you know well enough that it is just as illegal for you to give up Poverty as to give up Chastity. After throwing Poverty overboard it is easy enough to throw Chastity as well." [5]

SAINT FRANCIS AND HIS FOUR LADIES

And Francis' faithful followers continued to sing:

> *Povertate e nulla avere*   Poverty is having nothing.
> *e nulla cosa poi volere;*   And never to want anything
> *ed omne cosa possedere*   And to possess all things
> *en spirito de libertate.*[6]   In the spirit of liberty.

And he who had promoted the singing of the Lauda in the vernacular would, no doubt, have joined them vigorously.

When sick and blind and in great pain, he begged to be taken back to the Porziuncula, where he had first pledged his courteous allegiance to the Lady Poverty, and there to be laid naked on the bare ground.

> When you see me at my extremity, put me on the ground . . . and when I am dead, leave me there for such space of time as it takes a man leisurely to walk a mile . . . [7]

And so he died as he had lived, faithful to his Lady.

There is a prayer attributed to Francis:

> O my dear Lord Jesus, have pity upon me and upon my Lady Poverty, for I am consumed with love for her, and can know no rest without her. Thou knowest all this, my Lord. Thou who didst fill me with the love for her. But she sitteth in sadness, rejected of all; she, the Mistress of Nations is become as a widow;—the Queen of all Virtues is become contemptible.

This is not the young Francis confidently entering the lists for his Lady, but an older and wiser knight who had learned to recognize the strength of his adversaries.

The Lady Clare & his daughters

IT seems that the celibate Saint Francis bound by vows of chastity, may nevertheless have been drawn by a domestic dream of a wife, a family, and a household as is shown in the following story. Living one winter in a hermitage, he was beset with temptations of the flesh, whereupon he rushed out into the snow and fashioned seven snow heaps. "Behold," he said,

This larger heap is thy wife, these be two sons and two daughters, and the other two be a serving man and maid. Now bestir thee and clothe them, for they be perishing with cold. But if manifold cares on their behalf trouble thee, then be thou careful to serve the One Lord.

Thus—says his biographer Bonaventura—"he extinguished the fire of lust." Maybe so, but perhaps the most touching aspect of this story is that it goes so far and so naïvely beyond the burning "temptations of the flesh" reported by other frustrated monastics. The longing expressed here is for the intimacy and warmth of such a home as he had known in his childhood (and that he had vowed to abjure in the single-minded service of his Lord). It was this need to concentrate his efforts and not a disdain for sensuality as such that induced Francis to set out to implement literally every word of the gospel:

SAINT FRANCIS AND HIS FOUR LADIES

> If any man come to me and hate not his father and mother and wife and children and brethren and sisters, yea, and his own life also, he cannot be my disciple.[1]

This he understood to mean just what it says, and it was what he demanded of himself and those who joined his order. Such literalness in turn would make him say

> All talk with women is worthless except only in the way of confession or the very brief admonition that is customary.[2]

And on being told that new convents of sisters were being instituted in great numbers, he exclaimed,

> God has taken away our wives and now the devil gives us sisters.[3]

One day the Lord Ugolino, Bishop of Ostia, who was devoted to these cloistered women and perhaps sensed Francis' discomfort concerning them, said to him, "My brother, let me commend these ladies to you." Then Saint Francis "with a merry look" replied,

> That's right, father, in the future they shall not be called "lesser sisters" [*suore minori*] but "ladies" as you now term them in commending them to me.[4]

There may be a number of connotations of the word *ladies* but it is the term which, at that time, elevated women to an intrinsic dignity and freed them from the subservience of *sisters*.

But the remarks cited are, as it were, official statements to be heard by his brothers to strengthen them in their resolve to remain celibate and unencumbered by the demands of human relationships. As to individual members of the female sex, Saint Francis is on record as having stated that in all the world there were only two women's faces that he could claim to recognize, since his

THE LADY CLARE

habit was to lower his eyes when obliged to speak to women. It is said that these two known faces were those of the Lady Clare and the noble Matron, Jacomina da Settesoli. The latter had befriended him in Rome on one of his early journeys, and their friendship was maintained until he lay near death. At the Porziuncula he sent for her, and she arrived with her sons and a large retinue to bid him farewell. However, Francis always referred to her as Brother Jacomina, which may suggest something of her commanding stature and of the fraternal nature of their relationship.

And the face of Clare? Once when preaching to the Cardinals in Rome, "he showed them most skilfully" how in them "the glory of the Church should shine forth as in the face of a woman." It would seem, then, that Francis was aware of a possible perfection of the other-sexual in both men and women. Another popular legend relates how Francis and Brother Leo were returning from Siena, tired and troubled, and were resting by a well. Francis, who had been looking down into the water, after a time raised his eyes and smiled and said,

> Brother Leo, what do you think I have seen here? "The moon, father, which is reflected in the water." No, Brother Leo, not our sister Moon, but by the grace of God, I have seen the true face of the Lady Clare, and it is so pure and shining that all my doubts have vanished.[5]

Perhaps it was precisely clarity that he looked for in Clare Faverone, who was the oldest daughter of a noble house in Assisi. She was born in 1194 and was therefore twelve years younger than Francis. Her home was said to have been on the great piazza in the center of the city, and she belonged to a generation of young women who followed the dramatic career of Saint Francis from a distance, although some of them may have been influenced by his preaching. It is reported that she, however, was so singularly moved by his example and his message that she went with a friend to see him "secretly so that no one should see her" and that she listened to him "with utmost fervour." This secrecy was necessary, for since Clare was beautiful, the question of her marriage "to some great and powerful lord of her own rank" was being pressed by her family and relations. She is described as a young girl of intelligence, gaiety, and piety. Her "face was oval, her forehead spacious, her colour dazzling, and her eyebrows and hair very fair."

Saint Francis' early relationship to Clare is described for us by Celano, his first biographer.

> He, God's huntsman, was minded to snatch this noble booty from the world and to offer it to his Master. And so he visited her many times and she visited him.

It was Francis' desire, again according to Celano,

> that the dust of worldliness should not dim the mirror of Clare's immaculate spirit . . . and for this reason he hastened to draw her away from the darkness of the world.

The idea of Saint Francis as a "huntsman," "snatching booty" from the "darkness of the world" is one example of the kind of thinking that attempted to make him comprehensible after his death and resulted in the ironies of the memorials raised in his name.

He did persuade her to join his order, however, and one night Clare abandoned her home and her relatives' hopes for her future and met Francis and his brothers at the Porziuncula in the valley below Assisi. There he heard her vows of chastity, obedience, and poverty and with his own hands cut off her long golden hair.

THE LADY CLARE

He robed and veiled her, the first nun of his second order: women dedicated to monastic life.

One must pause here to marvel at the audacity of such an act on the part of the leader of a tiny new order. True, he had been given sanction by the Pope to form a group of "friars mendicants" to preach the simple gospel of repentance and rededication to Christ. But surely in this permission lay no mandate to start an order of religious women. At this time the "friars minor" were only a handful of men. To "snatch this noble booty from the world" was an affront to the nobility of Assisi and a threat to the accepted premise that women, and especially beautiful virgins of good family, were highly valued property. Possibly he had the sanction of the Bishop of Assisi because this prelate was friendly to the order from the beginning, but we have no evidence to support this assumption.

Clare went to live at San Damiano, and there other women joined her in the cloistered life which she maintained for forty-two years, outliving Francis by thirty years. She became the first abbess of a large world order of nuns, who still proclaim their unswerving allegiance to Saint Francis by calling themselves "Poor Clares."

What do we know of Saint Clare's relationship to Saint Francis? She speaks of herself repeatedly as "the little plant of our Father Saint Francis," and she makes it quite clear that she expects that she herself and her sisters will continue to be nourished by his care according to his explicit promise to her. For he had said,

> I will hereby promise on behalf of myself and my successors forever to have for you the same diligent care and special solicitude as for the brethren.[6]

As the order of friars grew, however, the responsibility of constantly caring for the "Poor Clares" (who were under vow of strict poverty and yet restrained from wandering and begging) became a burden of which the brothers would gladly have been relieved. But although the Church authorities repeatedly offered Clare a mitigated rule, she was adamant in maintaining this bond of dependence. She may have felt intuitively that this "caring" was in itself good for the fraternity. In any case, she clung to the literal meaning of her vow of poverty with a tenacity which reflected her complete dedication to Francis, determined to remain his little plant to the end. On her death bed she kissed the document sent to her by the Pope in which he assured her and her order of their right to adhere to strict poverty and to maintain their ties with the friars—a dispensation allowed only to her and her sisters at San Damiano.

She had asked for

> two honest lay Brothers of holy life to help us in our poverty even as we have always had through the courtesy of the said brothers.[7]

This she received, but Pope Gregory's letter to the friars after Francis' death is less chivalric in tone.

> I commit the charge of these women to you and your successors, forever. Take heed that you bestow on them such solicitude and care as a good shepherd does on the lambs of his flock and we place you under strict obedience to carry out this command to the letter.[8]

But why, we may ask in retrospect, had Saint Francis persuaded Clare in the first place that he needed her to carry out his particular mission to the world? Saint Benedict had created an order of women, a sister organization to his monastic order. But Benedict may well have been motivated to do so because of his devotion to his own sister, Scholastica. Saint Francis knew the Benedictine nuns near Assisi and committed Clare to their charge

THE LADY CLARE

after she had made her vows in his presence. The involvement of women in his work seems to have been of great importance to him, and Clare may have sensed this need. We can only surmise what her motivations may have been in giving up her privileged life to assume one of dedicated poverty under Saint Francis' rule. Yet their story indicates that she understood him and his work perhaps more truly than anyone else.

Medieval noblewomen were placed in a unique position by the changing social mores of their times. Where the martial spirit had dominated and indeed had been vital to survival during the constant warring that prevailed, a new era, more attuned to social and mercantile concerns, was dawning. The itinerant, competitive, often brutal lives that men were still forced to live as fighters laid the burden almost wholly on women of repesenting the aesthetic, the warmly solicitous, the more gracious aspects of life to balance the scale and make possible a creative style of living. Courtly ladies in the castles of the nobility, surrounded by knights, who knew only fighting and were free of all family ties, became idealized representations of all feminine virtue and beauty. They sensed the need, knew their powers, and responded according to their own ideals of conduct. It is possible that Clare, daughter of a noble house, was aware of the role that she and her cloistered ladies played in the lives of mendicant friars, lives given to constant wandering, with no place as their physical home.

Saint Clare speaks of Francis as "after God, the charioteer of her soul." This is the heroic, chivalric language of medieval imagery. But she used other images which are more childlike and suggest that Francis combined for her not only the attributes of a loving father but also those of a nourishing mother, being a source of both spiritual and sensual sustenance. A dream has survived:

> The Lady Clare also told that once she had seen St. Francis in a vision and she was bringing him a jug of hot water and with this she was ascending a long stairway, but so easily that it was as though she walked on the level earth. When she reached Saint Francis, he bared his breast saying: "Come, take and drink." And having sucked the Saint exhorted her to do so again: which doing what she sucked was so sweet and delightful that she could in no way describe it. And having sucked, that roundness, or the mouth of the pap from which the milk flowed remained in the mouth of blessed Clare; and if taken in the hand what had remained in her mouth seemed something bright and shining in which all could be seen as in a mirror, in which she saw her own reflection.[9]

This spiritual and yet also sensual dream language was not foreign to Clare's age. For had she not heard of the marvelous appearance of the Holy Virgin to Saint Bernard as he was reciting the "Ave Maria Stella" before her statue, when the Queen of Heaven had placed three drops of milk right from her breast into

THE LADY CLARE

his mouth? Dante recalls this miracle with awe in his *Paradiso,* and the story must long have been well known. But, of course, Clare's dream adds a new element to feminine sublimation in that she retained in her mouth her master's organ of nurturing and "saw her own reflection in it, as in a mirror." To this end she endured the privation of poverty with courage and tenacity, she cultivated humility (not an easily won virtue for the beautiful and intelligent), she made herself beloved for her practical solicitude toward her sisters in the cloister and seems to have evoked a devotion that convinced one and all of her complete saintliness.

In a letter written to Clare by Pope Gregory in 1228, he says,

> For ourselves, we can say you are our joy and consolation in all the cares and anxieties which continually oppress our heart.

Francis might have echoed this statement, but he expressed his love differently. He fully accepted the parental responsibility for this lovely young girl of eighteen whom he had selected to become the first abbess of his second order. She had taken her vows of chastity, poverty, and obedience in his presence—and obedience meant, first of all, obedience to him as the founder of the order. His first responsibility, in turn, had been to make ready the little cloister and chapel of San Damiano for her use and that of the women who soon joined her. San Damiano is a simple and beautiful little convent, surrounded by cypress trees, and remains today the most eloquent monument to the early spirit of the Franciscan movement.

One is led to suppose that some kind of a daily rule or routine was adapted by Clare from that of the Benedictine sisters with whom she had lived while Saint Francis prepared San Damiano. But Clare's rule was more rigorous, imposing a stricter discipline than that of the Benedictines, demanding minimal clothing of great simplicity, exacting manual labor, and requiring fasting and close adherence to hours of worship and prayer. But it was felt that these noblewomen could not go begging around the countryside or the cities of medieval Umbria without courting scandal, and for their support the help of the friars, as well as the services of lay sisters, was mandatory. And they needed priestly ministration and the teaching and preaching of the brothers.

Beyond these necessities it is reported that on one occasion Saint Clare could not refrain from expressing a feminine wish.

> St. Francis, when he abode at Assisi, ofttimes visited St. Clare and gave her holy admonishments; and she having very great longings to eat once with him, and thereto beseeching him many times, he was never willing to give her this consolation.

Could Saint Francis at that time have known about her dream? Whether he did or not, he may well have sensed a hidden intensity in her simple wish to share a meal. But he let the community decide.

> . . . wherefore his companions perceiving the desire of St. Clare said to St. Francis: "Father to us it seems that this severity is not in accordance with Divine charity, in that thou hearkenest not to Sister Clare, a virgin so holy and so beloved of God, in so small a matter as is this of eating with thee; and the more so considering that she through thy preaching abandoned the riches and pomps of the world; and of surety, if she asked of thee a greater boon than this, thou oughtest to grant it to thy spiritual offspring." Then St. Francis made answer: "Doth it seem to you that I ought to grant her prayer?" The companions replied: "Yea, father; it is a fitting thing that thou grant her this grace and consolation." Then St. Francis said: "Since it seemeth so to you, it seemeth so also to me. But to the end that she may have the greater

THE LADY CLARE

consolation, I desire that this meal be eaten in St. Mary of the Angels, because she hath been long shut up in St. Damiano, and thus will she have joy in beholding the Place of St. Mary, where she was shorn and made the bride of Jesus Christ; and there will we eat together in the name of God." Accordingly, the day thereunto appointed being come, St. Clare went forth from the convent with one companion, and accompained by the companions of St. Francis, came to St. Mary of the Angels, and after she had devoutly saluted the Virgin Mary before her altar, where she had been shorn and veiled, they took her to see the Place until the dinner hour was come. And, in the meantime, St. Francis caused the table to be set upon the bare ground, as he was wont to do. And when the dinner hour was come, St. Francis and St. Clare sat down together, and one of the companions of St. Francis with the companions of St. Clare; and thereafter all the other companions sate them humbly down at the table. And, at the first dish, St. Francis began to speak of God so sweetly, so highly and so marvellously, that abundance of Divine grace descended upon them and they were all rapt in.

And such is the power of the exalted wish that

While they were thus rapt, with eyes and hands raised to heaven, the men of Assisi and of Bettona and they of the district round about, saw that St. Mary of the Angels, and all the Place, and the wood which was then hard by the place, were burning fiercely; and it seemed to them that there was a great fire which encompassed the church and the monastery and the wood together, for the which cause the men of Assisi ran down thither with great haste to quench the fire, believing that verily everything was burning. But when they reached the Place, they saw that there was no fire at all, and they went in and found St. Francis and St. Clare and all their company rapt in God, through contemplation and sitting about that lowly board. Whereby they understood of a surety that that had been Divine fire and not material, the which God had made to appear miraculously to show forth and signify the fire of Divine love wherewith were enkindled the souls of those holy friars and nuns; wherefore they departed thence with great consolation of heart and holy edification. Then, after a long while St. Francis and St. Clare, together with the others returned to themselves and being greatly comforted with spiritual food they gave but little thought to bodily food; and so, that blessed meal being ended, St. Clare, well accompanied returned to St. Damiano.

It seems that Saint Clare may have proved herself in a very special test, for on her return her nuns greeted her with relief

and had great joy, in that they feared lest St. Francis should have sent her to rule some other convent, even as he had aforetime sent Sister Agnes, her holy sister, to be abbess of Monticelli in Florence; and St. Francis had once said to St. Clare: "Hold thyself in readiness, that, if need be, I may send thee to some other place;" whereto she as a daughter of holy obedience had made answer: "Father, I am ready to go whithersoever you shall send me;" and therefore the nuns rejoiced greatly when they received her back again; and from thenceforward St. Clare abode in much consolation.[10]

The legends indicate pretty constant communication between San Damiano and the Porziuncula, and in fact the distance between them is not great. But we may well imagine that the kind of visiting just described was unique. The incident, in fact, must of a certainty have taken place before the final rules of closure for the nuns had been enjoined. Indeed, the long introduction to the story indicates that it was in a way profoundly significant; for it seems that Saint Francis, as was his wont, settled a matter of deep inherent conflict with a dramatization of utmost simplicity which was felt by all participants to be an elemental event.

THE LADY CLARE

That Francis held Clare's judgment in high regard is clearly shown by the story of his seeking her advice as to the direction of his life work. After years of wandering and itinerant preaching, he began to feel attracted to the life of prayer—"the life of angels," as he called it—in some remote hermitage. So, as the story explains, he sent brother Masseo to the two friends whom he trusted most, the Lady Clare and Brother Sylvester, requesting them to pray and then advise him concerning his calling.

The description of Masseo's return gives us another glimpse of the ever-courteous Francis, for although he was no doubt anxiously awaiting the verdict as to the pattern of his life's work, he first greeted his messenger with tender consideration for the long and dusty journey. After an initial embrace Francis washed Masseo's feet and hands and then fed him solicitously. Only then did he take him aside to a quiet place to receive his message, which was that his "mission was to preach the Gospel for the salvation of souls." This injunction he accepted as final, and he received it with the immediate response, "Let us go forth in the name of God." The quiet of Clare's cloister encouraged clear judgment, and she was undoubtedly right for many good reasons. This intelligent and capable lady perhaps felt rather strongly that since her restricted role as a woman was to remain firmly "planted," even cloistered, then indeed her brothers belonged out in the world where so much work was to be done.

Later, however, San Damiano also became a refuge for Francis when illness made his difficult life work more and more impossible. During the early months of his last illness, he spent a long period of time in a little hut in the garden of the convent. It was for the sisters a great privilege to care for him. Clare's strict rule for the nuns mellows visibly when she speaks of caring for the ill, and her charitable admonitions serve well to indicate what convent austerities in the thirteenth century in cold Umbria may have been.

> Concerning sisters who are ill, the abbess, by personal observation and also by questioning the other sisters, shall carefully and diligently try to learn what is most necessary for the relief of their infirmities; whether medicine, nourishing food, or anything else; for which as far as her resources permit, she is bound in conscience charitably and compassionately to make provision. Indeed all the sisters are bound to cherish and serve those that are sick among them, even as they themselves would wish to be cherished were any infirmity to befall them. Therefore, make your necessities known confidently one to another. If an earthly mother cherishes her children according to the flesh, how much more should a spiritual sister cherish her sisters in religion!
>
> The sick shall lie on mattresses stuffed with straw and have feather pillows under their heads, and those that need them may likewise have woollen blankets over their feet and quilted counterpanes to cover them.[11]

This consideration for others had, no doubt, been sanctioned by Francis, who himself was so solicitous of his sick brothers. Since this, his last visit, followed the receiving of the stigmata at La Verna and since he was therefore unable to walk on his wounded feet without pain, she considerately made soft-padded sandals of leather for his comfort.

The secluded peace of San Damiano and indeed the presence of his beloved daughter seemed to foster in Francis his most soaring response to the glory of creation. Here he wrote his "Canticle of Brother Sun," in which he extends his characteristic courteous gratitude to the sun, the moon, the stars (which God makes *chiarite e belle*—Chiara—Clare—perhaps a not entirely intentional play on a well-loved name) and also to Sister Water,

THE LADY CLARE

Brother Fire, and Mother Earth. This poem of praise in Italian has an established place in the history of world literature—and indeed, it would have been quite out of character for Francis to have written verse in any language but that of the simple people. This, of all poems, deserves a page by itself.

Unfortunately for us, many of Saint Francis' writings are apparently lost. It is recorded that after leaving San Damiano for Riete, where the Bishop had sent for him to receive treatment for his eyes, he wrote many more poems which he sent to Saint Clare. These must have been composed after the painful and unsuccessful cauterization of his face and ears, when he was blind and in great pain. They have never been found.

In his last days, when he was dying at the Porziuncula and knew that he would not see Clare again, he sent her a "Last Will," which closes with the words:

> And I beseech you, my Ladies, and I exhort you to live always in this most holy life and poverty. Keep close watch over yourselves so that you never abandon it through the teaching or advice of anyone.[12]

These are firm, stern words of admonition, the last official words of a father to his "little plant" and those in her care. And she was obedient, holding unswervingly to her promise of poverty in the literal sense that she knew Francis had intended, for she understood perhaps better than all but a few of the brothers how significant his "marriage" to the Lady Poverty had been.

There were other messages, however, which he sent to her in those last days—among them the promise that she would see him again, which the friars fulfilled by bringing his body to San Damiano on the way to burial in Assisi. And there were also "sweet words of comfort like a song for their comfort and edification knowing them to be greatly afflicted by his suffering."

SAINT FRANCIS AND HIS FOUR LADIES

Canticle of Brother Sun

Most high, all powerful, good Lord,
Thine are all praise, glory, honor and all blessing
All things come of Thee, Most high
And no man is worthy to speak Thy name

Through all thy creatures Lord be praised
Especially through our Brother Sun
Who brings us day and illumines with Thy light
And he is gloriously radiant and splendid
Bespeaking Thee to us, Most High

Praise be to Thee Lord for Sister Moon and the stars
In the heavens Thou hast set them clear and precious and fair.

Praise be to Thee Lord for Brother Wind
And air and cloudy, clear and every kind of weather
By which Thy creatures all are nourished

Praise be to Thee O Lord for Sister Water
So useful, lowly, precious and chaste

Praise be to Thee O Lord for Brother Fire
By whom Thou dost illumine the night
For he is handsome and merry, sturdy and strong

Praise be to Thee O Lord for our Sister, Mother Earth
Who sustains and governs us
Bringing forth varied fruits, colorful flowers and grasses

Praise and bless the Lord with thankfulness
And serve Him in all humility.[13]

Our Lady Queen of Heaven

When I say Hail Mary, the heavens bow down, angels rejoice, Hell trembles, and the devils flee away. As wax melts in the fire and dust flies before the wind so at the invocation of the name of Mary the whole host of evil spirits is dispersed . . . danger, anguish, difficulty, call on Mary, think on Mary, let her not out of your heart or mouth.

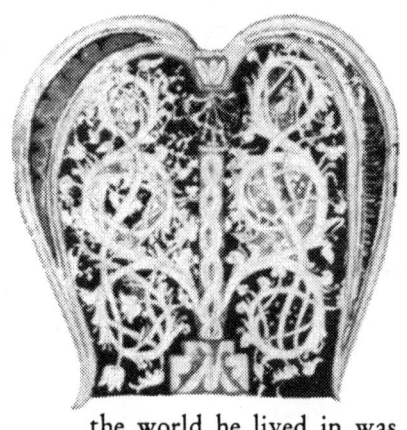

ARY was indeed in the hearts and mouths of medieval singers and writers and the words quoted above are attributed to the poet Saint Francis himself. But let us not be misled for this reason into the assumption that he was using figures of speech. He was a true son of the twelfth century, and the world he lived in was shared with rejoicing angels as well as fleeing and attacking devils. People saw visions, heard voices, witnessed miracles, and shared their astonishment with all who would lend an ear. Hell was visible, hot and smoldering in the craters of volcanoes. Anyone could describe an angel—long shining robes, a halo, bright wings—and even more vividly a devil—

black, rat-faced with fangs and horns and batlike wings. Saint Francis had personally to cope with them often when they molested his friars:

> It fell upon a day that one of those friars was offended with another and thought within his heart how he could accuse him and avenge himself on him; for which cause, while yet he cherished this evil thought, the devil, the door being opened, entered into the Place and set himself upon the neck of that Friar.[1]

But Mary was there also—Mary, the divine, once all-human mother of God—the powerful Queen of Heaven, who knew about life in the world and its complications, its "danger, anguish, difficulty," and who was near and compassionate to her children on earth. In fact, the figure of Mary played a powerful role in transforming the somber superstition of the Dark Ages into the illuminated and colorful era of Medieval Europe and the Crusades. Mary brought hope to people who were aware of a seemingly inevitable sinfulness which could only bring eternal damnation. And in this hope dedicated places for her worship were raised: eighty cathedrals and five hundred churches in France alone between 1170 and 1270, including incomparable Chartres.

No one can say how this began. Chivalry, knighthood, courtly love, the Crusades, and the contacts thus established with the Orient all played a part. Once introduced, however, the cult of the honor of the Virgin expanded and dominated the Catholic world to such an extent that the Church wisely, if reluctantly, joined in giving homage to the new queen. For she was a veritable queen—enthroned and crowned, gorgeously clothed, and ornamented with jewels: the Queen of Heaven. Her rule, in fact, became so supreme that the Trinity was for a while overshadowed by her splendor.

OUR LADY QUEEN OF HEAVEN

Saint Bernard, one of her earliest (1098) and most distinguished knights, addressed her thus:

> *O Saviour Virgin, Star of Sea*
> *Who bore for child the Son of Justice*
> *The Source of Light, Virgin always*
>   *Hear our praise!*
>
> *Queen of Heaven who have given*
> *Medicine to the sick, Grace to the devout*
> *Joy to the sad, Heaven's light to the world*
>   *And hope of salvation;*
>
> *Court royal, Virgin typical*
> *Grant us cure and guard*
> *Accept our vows, and by prayers*
>   *Drive all griefs away!* [2]

Translated into English, these verses lose the grandeur of the Latin original and even its claim to be poetry. The intention, however, remains clear. Saint Bernard is addressing a Universal Queen. All Cistercian churches were placed under her protection, while Bernard and his monks wore white in her honor.

Adam de Saint-Victor's hymn to her, written at about the same time, uses even more ecclesiastical phrases to establish her authority in the world of a Triune God:

> *Hail, Mother of Divinity!*
> *Hail Temple of the Trinity!*
>   *Home of the Triune God!*
> *In whom the Incarnate Word had birth*
> *The King! to whom you gave on earth*
>   *Imperial abode.*[3]

She was addressed as *imperatrix supernorum, Coali Regina, Aula regalis,* and neither the Church nor the court had at its disposal more imperious language.

OUR LADY QUEEN OF HEAVEN

Nevertheless, and this is the most surprising element in her worship, she was never out of the reach of the poor and forgotten "of whom God has made so many," for they could appeal unafraid to her divine motherhood and feel understood. Judging by the legends, Mary was most devoted to and cared untiringly for these simple people. They had no influence, no hope for preference in the courts of earth or heaven, and she became their regal advocate against the dominant masculine judgments from above.

Gaultier du Coincy, a monk, recorded fifty of her miracles in verse; and the oft-repeated tales which burgeoned would have filled volumes, so great was the need of people. They needed her to upset the natural order with its almost unbearable hardships as well as the exacting laws and restrictions of the social and ecclesiastical orders. She challenged death and saved the life of a robber simply by supporting him on the gibbet until it was clear to everyone that she meant him to live, for he had been faithful to her in his prayers. When Saint Peter asked for her help in saving the soul of a monk of Cologne who had led a scandalous life but was nevertheless Peter's responsibility,

> *Pierre, Pierre, our Lady said,*
> *With all my heart I'll give you aid,*
> *And to my gentle Son I'll sue*
> *Until I beg that soul for you.*

Her Son, of course, immediately on her approach,

> *Took her hand gently in His own;*
> *Gently placed her on His throne,*
> *Wishing her graciously good cheer!* [4]

and the request became a minor favor sure to be granted.

There is a moving tale of Mary visiting a dying beggar. A banker and a destitute woman, both being near death, summoned a priest at the same moment. The priest naturally went to the

Shrine "Vierge Ouvrante"

SAINT FRANCIS AND HIS FOUR LADIES

banker, but a clerk was inspired to visit the old woman, and well rewarded he was.

> *The clerk, well in these duties taught,*
> *The body of our Savior brought*
> *Where she lay upon her bed,*
> *Without a soul to give her aid.*
> *But such brightness there he saw*
> *As filled his mind with fear and awe.*
> *Covered with a mat of straw*
> *The woman lay; but round and near*
> *A dozen maidens sat, so fair*
> *No mortal man could dream such light,*
> *No mortal tongue describe the sight.*
> *Then he saw that next the bed,*
> *By the poor old woman's head,*
> *As she gasped and strained for breath*
> *In the agony of death,*
> *Sat Our Lady—bending low—*
> *While, with napkin white as snow,*
> *She dried the death-sweat on the brow.*

There was also a knight for whom she fought gloriously in the lists, while he himself heard mass in her honor in a wayside chapel.

She was supremely a lady of the twelfth century: knights were her champions, and her favor could be won by chivalric devotion and poesy.

> *To Mary Queen, who passes all compare*
> *Go, little songs! To her your sorrows tell!*
> *Nor Heaven nor Earth holds happiness so rare.*

Surely this is the tone of courtly love—of highest "courtesy." Mary was, then, Queen of Heaven, the great Patroness both of the court and the knights and of the poor and afflicted. The middle class—those who were scrambling up or desperately trying to keep from slipping down and were thus engrossed in the pursuit

OUR LADY QUEEN OF HEAVEN

of this world's goods—had less time, less inclination to her devotion.

It is difficult for us now in a puritanized and masculinized part of the world even to conceive of how the adoration of the Virgin permeated the medieval European world despite the initial efforts of the Church to curb excesses. Henry Adams, in *Mont Saint Michel and Chartres*, expresses the ubiquity of her presence in these words:

> These people knew the Virgin as well as they knew their own mothers: every jewel in her crown, every stitch of gold embroidery in her many robes; every color; every fold; every expression on the perfectly familiar features of her grave, imperial face; every care that lurked in the silent sadness of her power; repeated over and over again, in stone, glass, ivory, enamel, wood; in every room, at the head of every bed, hanging on every neck, standing at every street corner, the Virgin was as familiar to every one of them as the sun or the seasons. . . .
>
> How passionately they worshipped Mary, the Cathedral of Chartres shows; and how this worship elevated the whole sex, all the literature and history of the time proclaim . . . but still one cannot realize how actual Mary was to the men and women of the Middle Ages, and how she was present, as a matter of course, whether by way of miracle or as a habit of life, throughout their daily existence.

And with Mary was associated the ancient magic of the rose—the rose garden and the rosary. The rosette she inherited as her symbol from ancient mother goddesses of the Mediterranean world, the Eye Goddess of Syria, Isis, and Aphrodite, all "ladies of the rose." "Since," as Eithne Wilkins writes, "the rose was already a pre-Christian symbol of beauty, love, wisdom, and mystery, it is not surprising that it was from a very early time used as a symbol

of the beautiful, wise, and mysterious Virgin, Bride, and Mother."
In about the year 430 the poet Sedulius wrote of her in his *Carmen Paschale*:

> *As blooms among the thorns the lovely rose,*
> *herself without a thorn,*
> *The glory of the bush whose crown she is,*
> *So, springing from the root of Eve, Mary the new maiden*
> *Atoned for the sin of that first maiden long ago.*[5]

In medieval writings it was explained that the *Ave* of the "Ave Maria" was formed by the simple reversal of the word *Eva*, and thus Mary was acclaimed as the second, the new Eve. The Litany of Loreto, which lists all of her many titles, refers to Mary as *Stella Maris* ("Star of the Sea"), *Rosa Mundi* ("Rose of the World"), *Hortus Conclusus* ("Enclosed Garden") and has more recently added the title "Queen of the Most Holy Rosary." The significance of the interdependence of these ancient titles is too long and complicated a subject to deal with here. But the secret garden, the rose garden of Our Lady, is closely bound with the imagery of the garland of roses, the rosary. This "telling of beads," the counting of prayers with the aid and manipulation of small spheres between the fingers, was also a practice inherited from the Orient and the Near East and was probably stimulated like the rose garden theme, by the tales of homecoming Crusaders. Around such a Heavenly Personage all the mystery and symbolism of ancient pre-Christian female deities could converge and restore a unity of rational and emotional spirituality denied by the Judaic roots of Christianity.

What was Francis' position toward this veneration of the Virgin Mary?

As we have seen, the Lady Pica must have been an essential influence in his development, providing the atmosphere, the nour-

Coronation of the Virgin

ishment of his early years, sharing her Provençal background with him, and stimulating the formation of his aspirations and values. The Lady Poverty, his chosen wife, was, after all, his own creation and therefore, indeed, quite genuinely his lady on whom, as her true knight, his unswerving fidelity could be focused. The Lady Clare, whatever the first attraction may have been between them, became his sacred trust and by adoption a daughter on whom he could lavish his parental love. They were uniquely his Ladies, playing their roles in his drama, roles not to be repeated in anyone else's life. The Queen of Heaven, however, was every man's Lady, a pervasive figure and power, and we must try to see how Saint Francis wove her into his drama and found for her a role uniquely Franciscan.

That he was her knight and her petitioner is clearly shown by the prayer at the beginning of the chapter. He loved the Porziuncula or "little portion" which had been dedicated to her, "Saint Mary of the Angels," because it was said the angels sang there. It was his only home. He had repaired it with his own hands, and he pledged his brothers never to abandon it but there to center themselves in the care of the Virgin Mother.

He was her knight, belonging to a "supernatural order of chivalry," but more deeply because the grace of humility was his, he was her fool. Having set his course to obey literally the teaching of the Sermon on the Mount—to live in abject poverty, to be meek, to be pure, to hunger, to suffer—he set out to face the world around him with his message, his "good news." People having said, "he is either mad or he is a saint," finally agreed that he was indeed a saint; but to be a saint on his terms, one had also to be a bit mad—a fool for God.

This nature of his relationship to the Virgin Queen is perhaps most truly suggested by the contemporary story of the *Tombeor de Notre Dame.*

OUR LADY QUEEN OF HEAVEN

A street acrobat, in spite of his lowly position and ignorance of letters, is admitted into a monastery. There to his great distress he finds himself unable to take part in the liturgy of the services, "For he had learned no other thing—than to tumble, dance and spring." But his lack of all book learning, which would have endeared him to Francis, was not to break his spirit.

> *No! By God's mother, but I will!*
> *She shall not think me here for naught;*
> *At least I'll do what I've been taught!*
> *At least I'll serve in my own way*
> *God's mother in her church today.*
> *The others serve to pray and sing;*
> *I will serve to leap and spring.*

He proceeds to strip off his gown but keeps on a jacket, soft and thin, to tumble in. Then after again appealing to her grace:

> *Lady, who never yet could blame*
> *Those who serve you well and true*
> *All that I am, I am for you,*

he begins his performance "jumping high and low and in and out." He tires finally and pledges his return with his "tricks to make you laugh."

But he has been observed by a spying monk who rushes off in hot haste to inform his superior about this impiety. The following day they both hide to watch, and again he tumbles for his Lady until he falls exhausted and unconscious. And then:

> *The Abbot strains his eyes to see,*
> *And, from the vaulting, suddenly,*
> *A lady steps—so glorious—*
> *Beyond all thought so precious—*
> *Her robes so rich, so nobly worn—*
> *So rare the gems the robes adorn—*
> *As never yet so fair was born.*

SAINT FRANCIS AND HIS FOUR LADIES

The Lady Queen arrives with ranks of angels to restore her jongleur:

> *And the lady, gentle, true,*
> *Holds in her hand a towel new;*
> *Fans him with her hand divine*
> *Where he lies before the shrine.*
> *The kind lady, full of grace,*
> *Fans his neck, his breast, his face!*
> *Fans him herself to give him air!*
> *Labours, herself, to help him there!* [6]

The tombeor's playful kind of worshipful service was precisely in Francis' style—humble and yet courageous, generous to the point of physical exhaustion, joyous and certain that doing what he could do best would bring the most direct and maternal acknowledgment from above. Yet his devotion to Our Lady never replaced for Francis, as it did for many, his stark focus on the Cross, never since those early days in San Damiano when the voice had issued from the crucifix saying, "Francis, rebuild my house which as you see is in disrepair." It was the passion of Christ the Son which became the model of his life and the source of a brotherhood with all living things.

And, indeed, when he had done his duty by preaching this love to his fellowmen and, being weary and ill, realized that he had little longer to live, he retired to Mt. La Verna. There the miracle of the stigmatization took place—his hands and feet and side were marked with the wounds which Christ had received on the cross.

Having thus been so singularly distinguished over all other men—for there had been no saintly precedent to follow—had he not achieved a unique kind of sonship to the Virgin Mother? And this sonship—as that to his own mother most probably had been—remained both playful and devoted.

When Saint Francis was at the mountain hermitage in Greccio

OUR LADY QUEEN OF HEAVEN

and it was winter, he wished to celebrate the feast of Christ's birth for his brothers and the simple people who lived in the valley near them. So he had a stall built and brought there an ox and an ass and some sheep with hay for them to eat. And there he placed a manger with the figure of a child in it. Then he sent out to the villagers a message to come at midnight on the eve of Christ's birth and share their worship with the friars. They willingly trudged up the mountain with lanterns, and there they saw the crude crèche he had prepared for them, and they praised God.

> Greccio was transformed almost into a second Bethlehem and that wonderful night seemed like fullest day to both man and beast for the joy at the renewing of the mystery.[7]

Thus the first Christmas crèche came into being; and it seems that Francis had arranged it in such a spirit that the presence of

The Nativity

OUR LADY QUEEN OF HEAVEN

the Holy Virgin was taken for granted by all, even as everybody was reminded by the simple setting that the Queen of Heaven was on earth a lowly peasant woman whose companion throughout life had been poverty.

ARTIST~SAINT

PERHAPS we have now highlighted the significance of the four ladies for whom Saint Francis so courteously made space in his life; and we can come back to the fact that he was in an extraordinary way a man who could accept in himself a sensitivity we usually associate with femininity as well as a playfulness we ascribe only to children. And, indeed, the small boy who grew up in the Lady Pica's care continued to dream, to play, and to sing, maintaining a childlike reverence for all created things. The grown man, then, persistently stressed the joy of life itself even as he seemed to express it in every gesture. To a brother of melancholy appearance he said,

> Why do you make an outward show of sorrow and sadness for your sins? Keep such sadness between yourself and God, and pray to Him that, by His mercy, He

SAINT FRANCIS AND HIS FOUR LADIES

may spare you and restore to your soul the gladness of His salvation which you have lost through sin; but before me and others try always to be joyful, for it is not fitting that a servant of God should show before his brother, or others, sadness or a troubled face.[1]

And the legends tell us that in the warmth of his presence, people, animals, and things all flourished. They say that once in his travels he visited the hermitage on Mount Subiaco where, years earlier, Saint Benedict had lived. There Saint Benedict had planted a thorn hedge so that when assailed by temptations of the body he could tear his flesh with the thorns and thus thwart the evil one.

Saint Benedict rolling himself in thorn bushes

On Saint Francis' arrival the ancient thorn bushes burst into bloom.

Miracle or metaphor?—but what a story by which to be remembered! Now that we seem intent on destroying our world with alarming efficiency, it is no wonder that Saint Francis' inclusive reverence for all created things challenges our attentiveness again.

Almost habitually, we visualize Saint Francis as a small brown-clad figure with a bird, and indeed, he loved his "sisters the birds." He preached to them, and they listened—usually. But of all the birds his favorite was the meadowlark.

> Therefore Brother Francis loved also above all birds the bird which in everyday language is called the crested lark, and he said of it: "Sister lark has a hood like us and is an humble bird, for it goes willingly along the wayside and finds a grain of corn for itself. . . . Its plumage is of the same color as the earth and is an example to us that we shall not have fine and colored clothes, but simple and plain." [2]

The swallows who twittered noisily when he preached on the piazza in Orvieto obeyed when he courteously asked them to be quiet so that he might be heard. His brothers describe how he would join the birds around the Porziuncula in their early morning song, and he recommended this practice as an offering of praise most apt to be heard at "heaven's gate." And the black raven who was his companion during his final retreat at La Verna was his special friend.

But few of these Franciscan legends are well known, and we must assume that Saint Francis is associated with the bird as a pictorial symbol rather than as an allusion to any particular event in his life. With his flair for dramatization he must have brought home in a most telling manner a symbolic meaning which birds and the flight of their wings have had in human imagination through the ages.

SAINT FRANCIS AND HIS FOUR LADIES

The ancient Greeks looked upon birds as divine messengers from the gods, conveyers of prophecy or warning. Indeed, Mercury, who made the wishes of the gods known to men, had winged feet. Icarus, who challenged this god-given privilege of flight with his man-made wings, was quickly destroyed for such hubris. And

respect for winged things is, of course, supported by the symbolism in the Judeo-Christian tradition. The dove who brought Noah an olive branch as token of renewed life on earth remains our symbol of peace. This same gentle, man-oriented bird is also depicted as God's messenger in graphic representations of New Testament events such as the Annunciation and the baptism of Jesus. The Third Person of the Trinity, the "Holy Ghost who over the bent world broods with warm breast and with ah! bright wings," is depicted descending toward men in the form of a dove. And are not the very angels and seraphim themselves winged?

ARTIST SAINT

If the serpent has universally represented what was doomed to stay on the ground, the bird has just as universally represented the soul's flight toward the heights where the gods dwell. Mythology and, indeed, anthropology bear out the prevailing idea that the special attributes of birds, flight, and song have symbolized liberation for earthbound man.

In many lands tales are preserved about specially endowed persons with the mystical gift of understanding the language of birds and occasionally the ability to fly. This powerful magic, according to the old stories, is denied to the forces of evil, the witches, sorcerers, and cruel giants. Only the pure in heart, heroes, and wise counselors are thus endowed. These tales have survived, no doubt, because to a child wings offer irresistible dreams of freedom and omnipotence, a magic which re-echoes in us at the sight of wild geese flying by.

The full name of Saint Francis' "little place," the Porziuncula, was Saint Mary of the Angels. For him birds and angels were always very near and familiar, and it is probable that he especially enjoyed being among the trees around the Porziuncula because there he could let the birds come near him. And perhaps he felt close to them because they gave of themselves so generously with much song and without words.

True teaching, teaching that molds or changes, is, as everyone knows, accomplished by living example. For how else can the very young learn except through the quality of life in the human matrix of their world? This strong response to precedent is never outgrown. But when the Great Teacher was preaching to the multitudes who gathered to hear Him, the form he used was the parable. Probably this use of "a short fictitious narrative of a possible event in life or nature" accounts for the long, clear memory of His preaching and its final survival in the amazingly consistent

ARTIST SAINT

scriptural record. The beauty of the imagery used, the down-to-earthness of the examples, the universality of the spiritual truth illustrated, all played their parts in engraving these parables on the memories of those who heard them and of those generations since who have read them.

There are those, no doubt, who would cite the technique of Socrates as the purest verbal method of inducing people to think clearly and honestly and thus commit themselves to truth. He was another kind of great teacher, a master of the dialogue, relentlessly challenging the intellectual youth of Athens and of today.

Of Saint Francis one would have to say that he tended to repudiate the intellectual so that he might bring about changed action through released feeling. He was a poet, some say, and his life a great poem; he was a troubadour and his life a splendid song. He was a *jongleur de Dieu* who turned the established world topsy-turvy by challenging accepted values and embracing poverty, simplicity, and humility—the three dread adversaries of mercantile security. And it is true that the inspiration of his life helped to move his era toward a flowering of song and poetry as well as of painting, architecture, and religious rejuvenation.

And yet little of what this eloquent man said has been preserved. Those who have tried to recount the content of his message were obviously carried away by the impact of his performance. He was inspired, they tell us, and spoke "as the Spirit gave him utterance" with "ardent gestures and movements." He taught, then, by demonstration, by movement, kinesthesis, touch—the very elements of drama. He was a master of the dramatic parable. Using the most elementary grammar of behavior, he would juxtapose his message against prevalent modes of action and startle his audience into an immediate recognition of eternal truths. And he did this in such a way that the dramatic action could be redescribed and

SAINT FRANCIS AND HIS FOUR LADIES

understood by the simplest of men.

Let us reconsider a few outstanding scenes to see how he brought home his point. His youthful friends after an evening of feasting troop into the city for further "revelry." He stops, standing still in his tracks, and refuses to go on. They are surprised, and he increases their confusion by stating, when mockingly asked if he is lovesick, "Yes, but the bride I will woo is nobler, richer and fairer than any woman you know." They jeer and leave him but were to remember and to spread the story when the bride turned out to be his Lady Poverty.

His father demands the return of money appropriated by his son for rebuilding San Damiano. Saint Francis in the presence of the bishop and his assembled court hands him the money and strips himself of every garment, since, as he said, his father had paid for them all. Thus, reborn and naked, claiming only God as father, he faced his home town and the world.

These scenes were undoubtedly spontaneous improvisations, but later he was to develop the use of his imaginative capacity to reveal truth in action. On one occasion he was invited to dine as the guest of his friend Cardinal Ugolino, Bishop of Ostia. Now Saint Francis always praised the special virtue of food collected as alms, since it had been given "for the love of God."

> At dinner time he went out as if by stealth for alms from door to door. And when he returned, my Lord of Ostia had already gone in to dinner with many knights and nobles. But the blessed Francis drew near and placed the alms which he had received on the table beside him, for the bishop desired the blessed father always to sit near him. And the Cardinal was a little ashamed because Francis had gone for alms and put them on the table; but he said nothing to him because of the guests. And when the blessed Francis had eaten a little he took the alms and sent a little to each of the knights and chaplains

of my Lord Cardinal on behalf of the Lord God. . . .
And some did eat but others put it aside out of their
great devotion to him. After dinner Ugolino told
Francis that such behavior was an embarrassment to his
host. But Francis defended himself and said, "The bread
of charity is holy bread which the praise and love of the
Lord God sanctifies." [3]

Whether the knights and chaplains immediately approved of such behavior could be debated, and whether or not we sense a sly, perhaps humorous reproof in it, it is certain that they would remember and tell the tale.

Sometimes, however, Francis had to remind his own brothers that poverty, simplicity, and humility were their chosen way of life.

It happened that on another Easter Day, in the convent at Greccio, the Brothers, in honor of the feastday and of one of the ministers who had come as a guest, had covered the table with a cloth and had set out glasses instead of the tin cups. A little before mid-day Francis came along and saw the whole preparation; he quietly crept out, put on an old hat which a beggar had left after him, and with a staff in hand knocked at the door just as the Brothers were taking their seats. His appealing voice was heard at the door: *Per l'amor di messer domenedio, faciate elimosina a quisto povero ed infirmo peregrino!* "For the love of God, give alms to this poor and infirm pilgrim!"

On the Brothers' friendly invitation Francis entered. He sat down on the floor by the fireplace, had a dish of soup brought to him and a piece of bread, and began to eat. None of the Brothers said anything, and none could get down a mouthful—it was hard enough to sit there with that finely spread table while Francis, like a male Cinderella, with his dish on his lap, crouched down in the corner. Soon Francis laid down his spoon and said: "Now I am sitting as a Friar Minor ought to sit! But when I came in here and saw the fine spread upon the table, I did not think I was with poor members of the Order that had to go every day and beg their bread from door to door!" The Brothers could stand it now no longer; some of them began to weep, others rose and went to Francis as he sat there.[4]

And Francis did not hesitate to teach the Pope himself a never-to-be-forgotten lesson. When he first went to Rome with his small band to obtain papal sanction for his new order, he went directly to where he knew the Pope would be and waited for him to pass in the hall. In general, cleanliness was not a virtue of mendicant friars in those days, and Thomas of Spalato writes of Francis, "His tunic was dirty, his person unprepossessing, and his face far from handsome." As the Pope approached, Saint Francis addressed him, but the surprised and disgusted pontiff merely told him to go and roll in the pigsty. It is told that Francis did just that and then returned to confront his astounded superior. Fanciful legend? Perhaps, but it lives and breathes Saint Francis and his usual wry way of disconcerting those with whom he had an encounter by acting his message out. And, of course, there is always in such behavior an element, if not of outright mockery, then of forceful irony, that exposes all symbols of righteousness and power. Some may even sense malice underlying the irony and the mockery. If so, it is a malice most artfully disguised and put to pedagogic use. Otherwise we know little about Francis Bernardone's possible faults because they have been withheld from us by those who would have us see him as all but divine. The real miracle of his life is that in spite of his biographers he still comes through to us as three-dimensional. We can be grateful for the perception of Cimabue, who painted a face which had known conflict, frustration, and pain as well as the peace that passes understanding.

Finally—what could have made his message more telling than

the very scene of his death. Naked, lying on the bare earth with his arms outstretched, he demanded of his brothers that they sing his exit.

In conclusion, we may consider what it is that can make both artist and saint inspiring, as well as upsetting, to their fellowmen —so that a truly integral combination of the two remains unforgettable for generations.

The artist's attitude of attention, his keen sensitivity to stimuli from the sensory universe make him more open than others to perceptions that can be woven into a living whole—as sound—as image—or as idea expressed in word or in performance. This capacity to attend to the moment, to apprehend the common world, and then to give it form in surprisingly new proportions and new meanings—that is his unique talent.

> *To see the world in a grain of sand*
> *And a heaven in a wild flower.*[5]

This, then, as Blake knew, is the secret: to see again and forever with the child's innocent eye, as if for the first time, and to communicate this experience to others so that they rediscover as never quite seen that way before what is all around all the time. This rediscovery becomes a startling, a refreshing insight and a new inception of life as though one for an instant made contact again with beginnings and perhaps at the same time with infinity.

It is the "peculiar business" of the artist, Bergson says, "to brush aside everything that veils reality from us, in order to bring us face to face with the real, the true." These specialists of the real behind the conventional norms of perception can stir us out of our pathetic striving for the security of habit.

The saint's desire, in turn, is to maintain at all times a sharp sense of communion with God. He "Practices His Presence." But since it is possible to find something of "His fairness in all created things," the infinite is in the immediate and in the finite, and demands, if we were but able to give it, full attention at every moment of being.

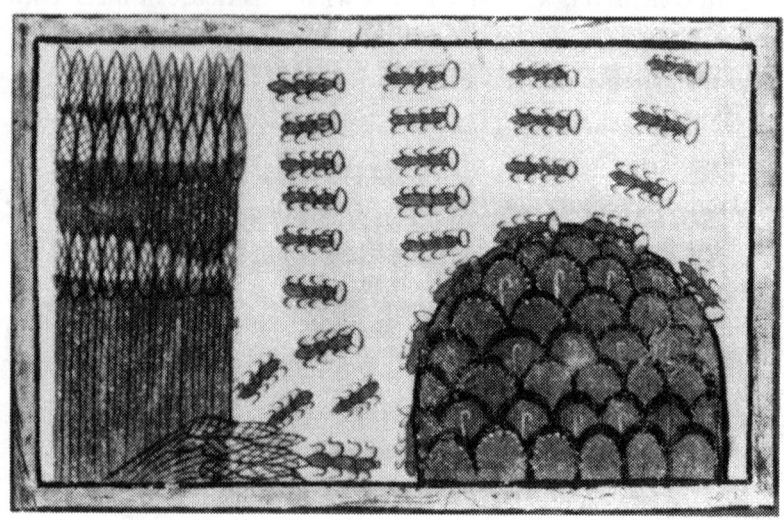

To recommunicate this aspect of the "good tidings" and to incorporate it in a memorable form—this then is the unique function of the saintly artist. He gives evidence of his fixed attention to the One by the abandonment of desire for what is merely comfortable either physically or spiritually. With an acceptance of poverty and pain, he lives confidently, for he has nothing that can be taken from him. In such freedom the most ordinary daily actions can be performed with simplicity and consecrated as loving service.

And artist and saint have something else in common. They must and do reconcile, at whatever cost of distress and frustration, the masculine and feminine in themselves. True, the male artist can always regain his masculine stature by embodying his tenderest insights in forceful and sometimes grandiose form, which he often does with a marked recovery of his vanity and his rebelliousness. For the woman the feminine propensity to bend with the gale will be allied with great firmness in truly creative mothering and all other creative activities. However, the saint who is an artist too must not only wed the two sides of our basic bisexuality which struggle for conciliation in all of us, but he must also manage a harmonious alliance of self-denying asceticism with receptive sensuality.

Francis Bernardone could be all of this: Knight Errant, troubadour, jongleur, dramatist, teacher, lyric poet—artist and saint. With his imaginative empathy he could reach out to those he met so that after a pause to speak with him on a donkey path in the Umbrian hills or in a cobbled Assisi alley, those he encountered remembered. Probably only a saint who was also a great servant of the sensory and who happened, too, to be a totally dedicated monk could proclaim so freely and joyously his devotion to the Ladies in his life.

One Franciscan follower, Pier Pettignano, had a dramatic vision—a vision as entrancingly apt as any "act" of Saint Francis.

> He saw in a vision a superb procession of Apostles, Saints and Martyrs, with the blessed Virgin at their head, all walking carefully and scrutinizing the ground with much earnestness that they might tread as nearly as possible in the very footsteps of Christ. At the end of this pageant of the Church Triumphant came the little shabby figure of Francis, barefoot and brown-robed; and he alone was walking easily and steadily in the actual footsteps of our Lord.[6]

Thus Francis, the "little poor one," came to be the very model of sainthood.

Prayer of Saint Francis of Assisi

Lord, make me a channel of thy peace That where there is hatred I may bring love That where there is wrong I may bring the spirit of forgiveness That where there is discord I may bring harmony That where there is error I may bring truth That where there is doubt I may bring faith That where there is despair I may bring hope That where there are shadows I may bring light That where there is sadness I may bring joy.

Lord, grant that I may seek rather to comfort than to be comforted to understand than to be understood to love than to be loved For it is by giving that we receive By self-forgetting that we find By forgiving that we are forgiven and it is by self-sacrifice that we awaken to eternal life

References

A GREAT BODY of literature, of course, exists on the life of Saint Francis. For the reader of English, however, there are a limited number of available translations of the sources. These include a recent translation of Thomas of Celano's early biography of Saint Francis by Fr. Placid Hermann, published by the Franciscan Herald Press; *Speculum Perfectionis or the Mirror of Perfection*, translated by Sebastian Evans; *Sacrum Commercium or the Converse of Saint Francis and his Sons with Holy Poverty*; *The Fioretti or Little Flowers of Saint Francis*, translated most recently by L. Sherley-Price; and *A New Fioretti: A Collection of Assisi Hitherto Untranslated*, by J. R. H. Moorman; *The Writings of Saint Francis of Assisi*, translated by Benem Fahy, O.F.M. A source book on the writings of Saint Clare with an introduction by Fr. Ignatius Brady, O.F.M., is entitled *The Life and Writings of Saint Clare of Assisi*.

In addition to these source materials there are a number of Lives of Saint Francis, that written by Sabatier in 1894 and translated in the same year by Louise Houghton being the oldest. The later (1912) *Saint Francis of Assisi* by Fr. Cuthbert is more accurate and less fanciful. A shorter *Saint Francis of Assisi* by John R. H. Moorman is excellent, and a life of Saint Clare, *Saint Clare of Assisi*, by Nesta de Robeck is most informative.

Of the many more "fictionalized" biographies which have been written in, or translated into, English, the *Saint Francis of Assisi* by a Dane, Johannes Jorgensen, is perhaps the best known.

SAINT AMONG SAINTS

1. E. W. Kemp, *Canonization and Authority in the Western Church* (London: Oxford University Press, 1948).
2. *Murtyrium Polycarpi*, chap. 18, trans. J. B. Lightfoot.
3. Arnaldo Fortini, *Assisi nel Medio Evo*. My translation.
4. *Dialogues of Gregory the Great*.
5. Matt. 3:4.

REFERENCES

6. Helen Waddell, *The Desert Fathers*, trans. from the Latin *Vitae Patrum* (London: Constable & Co., 1936).
7. *Ibid.*
8. *Ibid.*
9. *Ibid.*
10. *Ibid.*
11. *Ibid.*
12. John R. H. Moorman, *A New Fioretti.*
13. Evelyn Underhill, *Essentials of Mysticism.*
14. Jacopone da Todi, *Lauda.*

THE LADY PICA

1. *Paradisus Homo Amicus*, trans. Mother Adele Fiske, *Speculum* XL 3 (July 1965).
2. *Speculum Perfectionis or The Mirror of Perfection.*
3. *Ibid.*
4. Thomas of Celano, *Saint Francis of Assisi.*
5. Moorman, *A New Fioretti.*
6. Thomas of Celano, *op. cit.*
7. *Ibid.*
8. *Speculum Perfectionis.*

THE LADY POVERTY

1. *Speculum Perfectionis.*
2. *Ibid.*
3. *Ibid.*
4. *Ibid.*
5. Moorman, *A New Fioretti.*
6. Jacopone da Todi.
7. Thomas of Celano, *op. cit.*

THE LADY CLARE

1. Luke 14:26.
2. Thomas of Celano.
3. *Ibid.*
4. *Ibid.*
5. *The Fioretti or Little Flowers of Saint Francis.*
6. *The Writings of Saint Francis of Assisi.*
7. Nesta de Robeck, *Saint Clare of Assisi.*
8. *Ibid.*
9. *Archivum Historicum*, vol. 13, trans. Nesta de Robeck, Quaracchi, 1920.
10. *Fioretti or Little Flowers.*

REFERENCES

11. Fr. Ignatius Brady, *The Rule of Saint Clare: Life and Writings of Saint Clare.*
12. Rubric of Assisi M.S. 338: "Here begin the Praises of the Creatures which the Blessed Francis composed for the praise and honour of God, while he lay sick at San Damiano." Archivum Franciscanum Historicum, vol. 24. My translation.
13. *Writings of Saint Francis of Assisi.*

OUR LADY, QUEEN OF HEAVEN

1. Thomas of Celano.
2. Henry Adams, *Mont Saint Michel and Chartres.*
3. *Ibid.*
4. *Ibid.*
5. Eithne Wilkins, *The Rose-Garden Game: A Tradition of Beads and Balls* (New York: Herder & Herder, 1969).
6. Adams, *op. cit.*
7. *Fioretti or Little Flowers.*

ARTIST SAINT

1. *Speculum Perfectionis.*
2. *Ibid.*
3. *Ibid.*, as quoted by J. Moorman.
4. *Ibid.*, as quoted by J. Jorgensen.
5. William Blake, "Auguries of Innocence."
6. Nesta de Robeck, *Saint Clare of Assisi.*

List of Illustrations

WITH NOTES AND COMMENTS

OBVIOUSLY portraits of Saint Francis must postdate his lifetime. Even Giotto and the frescoes in the Upper Basilica of Saint Francis in Assisi were painted one hundred years after his death. Instead, I have elected for the most part to include only such visual material as Saint Francis himself might have seen. This I have found in old and precious illuminated manuscripts and in a few early works of art. There are two exceptions; the fresco of Saint Francis by Cimabue and that of the marriage of Saint Francis with the Lady Poverty attributed to Giotto and his school. Both are in the Lower Basilica of Saint Francis in Assisi.

The imaginative and childlike style of the illuminations and miniatures in these early manuscripts is of a simple and singing quality which, one senses, Saint Francis would have appreciated. In fact one Maius, scribe and miniaturist of the *Commentarius super Apocalypsum* listed below, writes into the manuscript a most Franciscan "exultate." "Let the faithful voice resound and shout aloud, aye, let Maius, small but eager sing in jubilation, melodiously sing, rouse the echoes and loudly call."

Manuscript and folio numbers are those assigned by the Pierpont Morgan Library, New York.

Letter F on book jacket and Title page. [M1, f112]

Frame on Contents page. [M98, f80v]

PAGE 6 / Birds, souls of saints. *Commentarius super Apocalypsum*. Beatus of Liebana. Written and illuminated in Leon, Spain, in 922 or 926. The scribe and miniaturist Maius states that it was executed at the request of Abbot Victor of the monastery dedicated to Saint Michael. [M644, f214]

PAGE 9 / Letter T. Bible. Latin. Manuscript on very large sheets of medium vellum written and illuminated in central Italy, possibly at Bobbio early in the twelfth century. [M392, f300v]

PAGES 10–11 / Dedication of a Book to the Virgin (detail). German

LIST OF ILLUSTRATIONS

School (Swabian). Fifteenth century. Tempera on parchment. [The Metropolitan Museum of Art, Gift of Sarah Gibbs Thompson Bell, 1939.]

PAGE 14 / Horned animal. *Bestiaire d'Amour*. Richard de Fournival, 1200–1250. Written and illuminated in northern Italy.
The popularity of the *Bestiaire d'Amour* is attested to by the fact that it exists in at least eighteen recorded manuscripts in addition to this one, as well as in a rhymed version by the author himself, and in Flemish and Franconian translations. [M459, f25]

PAGE 17 / Letter S. See note for page 9. [M393, f375 (detail)]

PAGE 20 / Stoning of Stephen. Lections of the Gospels for reading during the service of the Mass throughout the Church year. Written and illuminated for the Benedictine monastery of Saint Peter at Salzburg, Austria, by Custos Perhtolt in the second half of the eleventh century. [M780, f6v]

PAGES 24–25 / Adoration of the Lamb by the multitude. The miniature is painted on three horizontal zones: 1. Lamb of God holding cross in a medallion supported by the wings of the Four Beasts with human bodies on wheels. These are flanked by two groups of angels. In rectangle at right, an angel addresses John, holding an open book; 2. Twenty-one martyrs holding palm branches; 3. Four rows of saints, labeled: 144 sons of Israel. See note for page 6. [M644, f117–118]

PAGE 27 / A man on his knees begging for mercy. The nobility of the lion is such that it spares the life of those who entreat for mercy. See note for page 14. [M459, f26 (detail)]

PAGE 32 / Tomb slab of monk. French. [The Metropolitan Museum of Art, The Cloisters Collection, Purchase, 1930.]

PAGE 36 / Portrait of Saint Michael. Written and illuminated in Fayûm, Egypt, probably at Saint Michael's monastery at Sôpehes (Hamouli) in 974. [M607, f1v]

PAGE 39 / Letter T. See note for page 9. [M392, f300v]

PAGE 40 / Detail from Latin Psalter written and profusely illuminated probably at Lesner Abbey in Kent, 1210–1220. [M43, f9v]

PAGE 41 / Detail from Latin Psalter. See note for page 40. [M43, f9]

PAGE 45 / Sea-borne Knights. *Miracula sancti Eadmundi, regis et martyris; Passio sancti Eadmundi*. Saint Abbon of Fleury. Manuscript on vellum, written and illuminated in the Abbey of Bury Saint Edmund's, Suffolk, England, in the middle of the twelfth century. [M736, f7v]

PAGE 49 / Saint Francis of Assisi. Cimabue. [Alinari]

PAGE 51 / Animals. See note for page 14. [M459, f11]

PAGE 53 / Letter E. Psalter. Latin. Thirteenth century. Written and

LIST OF ILLUSTRATIONS

illuminated at Cologne, Germany. Exultate: A woman sits full face playing with two hammers on four bells hung above. [M94, f77]

PAGE 55 / Chansonnier Provençal. A page from a thirteenth-century manuscript written and illuminated at Padua, Italy. [M819, f190]

PAGE 57 / Knights in Battle. See note for page 45. [M736, f7v]

PAGE 58 / Lady and Lover. See note for page 14. [M459, f11]

PAGE 63 / Blanche of Castile, Saint Louis, author and scribe. *Apocalypse—Moralized Latin.* Early thirteenth century. Written and illuminated in France for Blanche of Castile and her son, Saint Louis. [M240, f8]

PAGE 66 / Wolf sniffing before a sheepfold. *Bestiary.* Latin. Written and illuminated in England in the twelfth century and given in 1187 to the Augustinian Priory of Radford by Philip, Canon of Lincoln. [M81, f25]

PAGE 71 / Letter H. See note for page 9. [M391, f54]

PAGE 73 / Marriage of Saint Francis and Lady Poverty. School of Giotto. Lower Basilica, Assisi. [Alinari]

PAGE 83 / Letter I. See note for page 9. [M391–3, f338]

PAGE 89 / Psalter. Latin. Thirteenth century. Written and illuminated in England. [M756, f9v]

PAGE 99 / *Commentarius super Apocalypsum.* See note for page 6. [M644, f209v]

PAGE 101 / Letter M. See note for page 9. [M393, f403v]

PAGE 104 / Shrine ("Vierge ouvrante"). French. Wood covered with linen, gesso, and gilt. [The Metropolitan Museum of Art, Gift of J. Pierpont Morgan, 1917.]

PAGE 109 / Gradual and Sacramentary for use in the Benedictine abbey of Weingarten diocese of Constance, Bavaria, Germany. [M711, f57]

PAGE 113 / Crucifix. Wood. Northern Italy. Twelfth century. [The Metropolitan Museum of Art, Fletcher Fund, 1947.]

PAGE 114 / The Nativity. Bible, New Testament Gospels. Latin. Written and illuminated in the Benedictine monastery of Saint Peter's at Salzburg, Austria, in the first half of the eleventh century. [M781, f133 (detail)]

PAGE 117 / Letter P. Bible, Old Testament, Psalms. Latin. Written and decorated in north England about the middle of the eighth century. [M776, f59v]

PAGE 118 / Saint Benedict rolling himself in thorn bushes to drive away temptation. His habit hangs on tree. *Dialogorum liberii Vita S.*

LIST OF ILLUSTRATIONS

Benedicti. Italian. Fifteenth century. Written and illustrated at the monastery of Santa Justina at Piacenza for the monastery of Saint Sixtus. [M184, f7v]

PAGE 120 / Caladrius—a lark white, perched on bed of sick man looking at him. This shows he will recover. See note for page 66. [M81, f60v]

PAGE 122 / Bible, New Testament Gospels. Tenth century. Written and illuminated in northwest France, probably in the diocese of Amiens. [M319, f123v]

PAGE 128 / Ants. See note for page 66. [M81, f31v]

PAGE 130 / Angel with horn. See note for page 6. [M644, f156]
The hand-lettered "Prayer of Saint Francis" was done by Elizabeth Gatchel Klein.

PAGE 140 / Peacock. "The Windmill Psalters." Written and illuminated in England. [M102, f2]

EU Authorised Representative:
Easy Access System Europe
Mustamäe tee 50, 10621 Tallinn, Estonia

www.ingramcontent.com/pod-product-compliance
Lightning Source LLC
Chambersburg PA
CBHW071359160426
42811CB00111B/2287/J